Built by Wendy
COATS & JACKETS

THE **SEW U** GUIDE TO MAKING OUTERWEAR EASY

Wendy Mullin
with Eviana Hartman

ILLUSTRATIONS BY BECI ORPIN

ADDITIONAL ILLUSTRATIONS BY DANA VACCARELLI

POTTER
CRAFT

NEW YORK

CONTENTS

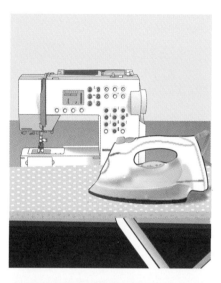

outer space

WHY COATS AND JACKETS ARE EASIER TO MAKE THAN YOU THINK

Some people say the most important building blocks of a woman's wardrobe are a little black dress and a great white shirt. While I certainly couldn't live without either of those, I think the real key to always looking stylish is the right mix of great coats and jackets. After all, unless it's the hottest part of summer, you usually need something to cover you up, and you only look as good as your outermost layer. There's arguably no other garment in which function and fashion play such equally crucial roles.

But the great thing about coats and jackets is that they don't just have to cover you up—they can really pull your look together. If you check out some of the street-style websites that insiders follow for inspiration, you'll notice that almost every one of the trendsetters in them is wearing a jacket or coat, working it into an overall look whether it's to jazz a simple outfit up, dress a fancy one down, or add a touch of tailored simplicity to a look full of piled-on accessories. Layering and seasonless dressing are a part of life these days: It's not just about buying one winter coat and one spring jacket anymore. We're busy running around from meetings to the gym to parties without a moment to spare, and we need that crucial piece to keep us feeling polished, comfortable, and ready for sudden changes in the weather (and our schedule). A jacket or coat is the most important part of this equation—and since it's the kind of piece you may end up wearing every day, it's a great billboard for expressing your personality through color, pattern, shape, and detail.

Best of all? Coats and jackets may look complicated and scary to sew, but when you break them down, they're not as tricky as they seem. They really just require the same techniques that you'd use for sewing a dress, shirt, or pants. My first foray into outerwear was inspired by a look at my mom's old black wool Pierre Cardin coat from the sixties, with big double buttons and curved pockets. I made a sort of straight overcoat that was constructed almost like a robe: It simply had a back, a front, sleeves, and a belt—no collar or anything! I lined it with a pretty floral fabric and even added some colorful trim on the hem. Oh, and it was bright pink—I would never spend a ton of money on a bright pink coat at a store, but when you're making such easy styles, you might as well make a statement piece, right? (That's another thing about making your own coats and jackets—they tend to be the most expensive clothes to buy, and you can really save money by doing it yourself. So why not test out your wildest ideas?)

As time went on, I got into making more sophisticated shapes in more muted colors. You can do the same and make yourself a wide range of outerwear to fit all your looks for every season, event, and mood. Why not try a brown faux-fur bolero jacket to throw on over jeans and a top by day and a silk-satin beaded dress by night? Or add a special touch to my tomboyish olive green anorak by sewing on vintage patches for a more authentic military look. Satisfy your boho side with a floral-print quilted-cotton shell jacket, or turn preppy cotton twill into a fitted golf jacket. With the skills you'll learn in this book, you can make ladylike looks (a Chanel-like dinner jacket in metallic-flecked bouclé with woolly trim or a cotton babydoll jacket with a satin-ribbon tie-front closure) or go in the opposite direction (a heavy-duty carpenter jacket in canvas with corduroy collar and pencil pockets, a woolly plaid hunting jacket with plenty of pockets, or a quilted nylon hooded vest for those chilly fall days). A boiled-wool poncho would be great for wearing around the fire while camping, while a cotton piqué Baja for the summer can easily be made in terry cloth for a great beach cover-up (just add a bit to the length). A round-shouldered jacket with a curved yoke around the body can be made two-tone for a graphic, mod twist, or used as a template for inserting ruffles. For a sophisticated alternative to a jean jacket, you might try a kimono shape in indigo ikat print with an asymmetrical wrap front. Inspired yet?

book smart

WHAT TO EXPECT

In this book, I have included three patterns—the fitted jacket, the basic jacket, and the straight coat—along with many different project ideas for customizing each one to create a wide range of styles. I picked these three basic patterns because they are templates that cover a range of silhouettes: The fitted jacket is slim, shaped, and waist-length; the basic jacket is straight and hip length with set-in sleeves; and the straight coat is longer with raglan sleeves. It's nice to have options between different types of sleeves and different fits. With these basic shapes, almost any coat and jacket can be made.

I have a host of designs with lining, and many without; some use various trims, while others have none at all. Whatever level of sewing you are at, you'll feel confident enough to make many of these projects. You also can customize them to your skill: Maybe you like the army jacket, but you want to make it in wool with a lining to challenge yourself. Or maybe you're a beginner, and instead of making a coat with a button front, you could substitute a self-belt, a robe-style wrap closure that means you don't have to worry about buttons and buttonholes. Don't think of any of the projects as strict guidelines—they're merely suggestions to get your creative juices flowing!

Before we get to the projects, though, I'll walk you through the basics of designing, preparation, supplies, patterns, cutting, and sewing as they pertain to outerwear, using secrets and shortcuts I've learned over the last two decades as a designer as well as a home sewer. There are plenty of differences between sewing coats and sewing clothes, but unless you're a total newbie, there's nothing to be intimidated by—you won't even need any special equipment or tools (unless you'll be working with leather). One thing you'll have to get used to is the process of sewing in linings, since most coats and jackets have them. When I first started, I would design my coats and jackets without them because they seemed too tricky, but later I learned that it's actually really easy to sew one in—plus you'll save time, because a lining hides all the unfinished seam allowances. (Not to worry, though, I do offer many options without lining, too—it can create a very cool look.) Also, working with heavier fabrics takes a little getting used to. A coat's worth of wool can be a lot of weight to move around, and if you don't have a lot of space on your sewing table, half of it ends up on the floor while you're sewing. I remember making a coat once and having to constantly lint-roll it because my dog's hair was getting all over the hem!

The last thing about making coats and jackets that tends to work slightly differently from other garments is the process of sewing and attaching trims and closures. I've found that sewing in separating zippers to make zip-front jackets is actually much easier than sewing an invisible zipper into a silk dress. As far as sewing buttons goes, you have to spend a bit more time creating a shank on each button to make room for the heavier fabric to fit under the button. Otherwise, coats and jackets are really (I swear) not that much different than sewing a dress or blouse— which is why you shouldn't be afraid to get creative. Think of my project ideas as a starting point, and again, feel free to mix them up however you like—substitute toggles for buttons, add furry fleece to collars, line a black wool peacoat with electric purple taffeta. The sky's the limit—now let's get sewing!

CHAPTER 1

TOP DESIGN

CREATING COATS AND JACKETS FOR ALL OCCASIONS

I ALWAYS GET EXCITED WHEN DESIGNING COATS AND JACKETS,

because it's the part of each collection where I get to think, "What do I really *need*?" Coats and jackets have to perform a function—keeping you protected from the elements and comfortable in the day's weather—but they also have to look and feel good. That's a lot of factors that have to fall into place for any given occasion, which is why I always find myself thinking up new coat and jacket ideas, and why I think it's a great idea to collect them as you would dresses or pairs of shoes. For example, I hated when I used to go out to parties and I didn't have the right coat to go over the dress I was wearing. Somehow, what I had was either the wrong color, fabric, season, or length; maybe it felt too stuffy, or maybe it just wasn't appropriate for the occasion.

When designing my collections, I always set aside some time to make coats so that I have it all covered: the perfect woolly day coat to wear on a cold fall afternoon while hitting the museums; a great lightweight cashmere tea-length coat with three-quarter sleeves for any fall evening occasion; and even a silk-linen coat for those breezy spring evenings. But I always include those few essentials that I can never seem to find in just the right proportion—a classic army jacket for trekking around town, a fitted wool peacoat that makes you look slender, a cotton golf jacket that's not cut like Gramps's old version. The basics are important, but I also like to design jackets and coats that are statement pieces: I love adding a bit of pizzazz to a basic outfit by throwing on a bolero jacket in a bright color, or a Chanel-style wool bouclé dinner jacket to spice up a pair of jeans and turtleneck.

While their construction is more elaborate than, say, that of a simple tube skirt, coats and jackets are incredibly versatile garments that lend themselves especially well to customizing. In this book, I have included three basic patterns that can translate into a vast array of styles. Believe it or not, these three simple templates are the basis for most of the jacket and coat styles in my collections. I use them season after season because they work!

Once I've figure out what I need in my wardrobe, I get down to the design process. For jackets and coats, it always starts with function—where I'll wear it, what time of year, and what features will make it look right and perform well. Let's say you need a great fall jacket to wear to work. OK, do you want a collar or a hood? Maybe a collar is more sophisticated. What sort of pockets and how many? What length? Maybe something that almost covers your skirt, if that's what you wear to work every day. Or maybe you'd prefer something shorter, if you tend toward pants and jeans and want to show off your long legs and move around freely. Once you sketch out your shape, you can get into finding fabrics. That's the fun part! Lastly, you'll choose trims. Cool doodads like zippers and buttons can make a huge difference in the overall look of your design.

the big three

JACKET AND COAT PATTERN SHAPES

In this book, I have included three different patterns: the fitted jacket, the basic jacket, and the straight coat. I chose them because they are such versatile starting points for creating a range of coat and jacket styles. You won't believe how different each pattern can become! Here's a look at the properties of each one.

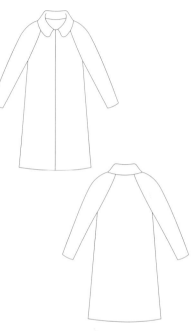

FITTED JACKET

The body-skimming princess seams make this jacket hug the body and contour curves in just the right way. The basic version of the pattern in this book hits slightly below your waist. I have included a stand-up collar that can be easily changed into different types of collars, or simply removed. This is an ideal pattern to create small, fitted jackets to wear over blouses.

BASIC JACKET

This jacket has a looser, straighter fit since it doesn't have princess seams as in the fitted jacket to sculpt the silhouette. The pattern is also slightly longer than that of the fitted jacket; it's designed to hit at the hips. This style is the perfect starting point for basic slim-fitting jackets. Included is a hood, a piece you can mix and match with the other jacket and coat patterns. Don't be afraid to try making a hooded straight coat or adding a hood to the fitted jacket, too!

STRAIGHT COAT

This knee-length, loose-fitting coat with raglan sleeves and a basic collar is a great template for a classic overcoat. The raglan sleeves, with their diagonal seams, lend themselves to variations that standard set-in sleeves do not. What does this mean? A set-in sleeve attaches at the shoulder, while the raglan sleeve attaches at the neck, so that the sleeve piece forms not only the sleeve but the shoulder as well. Having patterns for both set-in and raglan sleeves is essential to give you the tools for making all variations of all sleeves.

CONSIDERING YOUR SHAPE

Generally speaking, jackets and coats aren't as tricky to fit as, say, constructed figure-hugging dresses. Still, it's important to consider your size when working with (or altering) the patterns and style ideas in this book. You can play around as much as you want, of course, but keep in mind that some styles flatter different body types better than others.

Height

If a peacoat design is shown here hitting at the hip, you're welcome to make it full-length—but if you're Olsen-sized, that silhouette might overwhelm you. On the other end of the spectrum: For ultratall and long-waisted frames, what works as a hip-length jacket for most people might hit you at your natural waist and look strange.

Measurements

A jacket's shape can emphasize or conceal your figure. The lean and long-legged tend to look great in cropped styles; if you're self-conscious about your curves, a tailored, body-skimming hip-length look will create a streamlined silhouette. If you're insecure about your butt but love your sculpted calves, something midthigh length or lower will show off your favorite asset.

Details play a part, too. If you have broad, athletic shoulders and a larger chest, you might want to avoid an army-type jacket with big chest pockets, which might just make you look wide. Or you could just skip the pockets altogether. You can also move pocket placement around. For instance if you are short, maybe you should move the pockets up an inch or two so they hit in a place that is comfortable to put your hands in. Sometimes it's good to pin the pockets on before sewing to check their placement and move them to where they're flattering and functional.

The following guidelines are helpful suggestions for what flatters, but are by no means hard-and-fast rules. It's also key to keep in mind which styles you like, and what fits with your personal style and wardrobe needs. Also, each project in this book has multiple alternatives that give a totally different look with some simple pattern tweaks, so take a look at everything and stay open-minded!

Arms

If the sleeves of a coat are too long, they look dowdy, and if they are too short, the jacket can look like it doesn't fit, even if it's perfect everywhere else. I prefer sleeves that end about one inch (2.5cm) beyond the wrist, and the basic patterns reflect this measurement for the average person. Also, if a sleeve is too wide, it can look unflattering and unfeminine. I prefer slim-fitting sleeves, unless the style has looser sleeves that work with the body shape. It's good to try on your jacket or coat before finishing openings like hems and sleeves so that you can pin it at the ideal fit and make small alterations, like shortening or slimming, before it's a done deal.

BODY TYPE

Petite

General Guidelines: Above-the-knee styles are best, and you can pull off crazier styles and fabrics easily. Keep pocket and belt placement in mind; you may need to move things up. Especially for cropped styles, you may want to shorten the hem to get the proportion right.

Great Coat: Army of One

Also Try: Baby Bolero (just check the muslin length first)!

Curvy

General Guidelines: Body-skimming—not snug and super-sculpted—looks are easy to wear and slimming. Baggy, boyish styles hide lumps and bumps, but layer them over something streamlined so you don't look too shapeless. Solid colors tend to be most flattering on curves.

Great Coats: Scarf Coat, Jackie Jacket

Also Try: G.I. Jane, That's a Wrap

Athletic

General Guidelines: A-line and looser, flow-y shapes balance out broad shoulders. Face-framing collars and hoods also take focus away from the upper arms.

Great Coats: Kimono Chic, Perfect Peacoat

Also Try: Code Orange, Chic Poncho

Tall

General Guidelines: You may need to lengthen some styles, and lower pockets and belt loops, to get them to hit in the right place. You can pull off almost any length! Loud colors and wacky prints may come across as a bit overwhelming on larger frames, but confidence matters most, so go with your gut!

Great Coats: Go Speed Racer!, Column Coat

Also Try: Updated Jean Jacket, Paddington Coat

small wonders
DESIGN DETAILS

When designing coats and jackets, I like to make sure I cover certain details that will make it functional, such as providing pockets in a coat (who doesn't want a place to put their hands when it's cold?) or putting a hood on a beach cover-up (to help shield you from the sun). Generally speaking, for my line I try to stay pretty reality based and stick to the classics, but at times it's fun to experiment and combine different details. For example, why not a make a coat with trench-coat yokes out of rainwear fabric with peacoat buttons—it's like a pea-raincoat. Or you could try making an army-type jacket with epaulettes and lots of pockets, but in wool bouclé with trim, à la Chanel. Sure, we all can use a basic black wool-cashmere coat, but sometimes—like on a gray, sleeting January day—a girl just wants to rock a quilted Lurex poncho to cheer herself up (and there's no way you'll find *that* at the local mall).

NECKLINES, COLLARS, AND HOODS

All of the patterns in the book come with a simple jewel neckline and a stand-up collar, hood, and basic collar that are interchangeable. I will show you some ways in the different project sections to change the shape and size of the neckline features.

Using patternmaking skills, you can make these pieces bigger or smaller to tweak the style. (For a great primer on patternmaking, I recommend *Patternmaking for Fashion Design* by Helen Joseph Armstrong.) For instance, the hood pattern with this book is a basic-sized hood, but if you add a bit to the height, it can become a much looser, bigger, dramatic cloaklike hood. You can also add a drawstring so that it's more like a hoodie, or you add a tab at the neck for a classic, scholarly Pendleton-type look. (You can also make that hood pointed rather than rounded if you want to look like a witch, but I suspect you won't, unless it's Halloween!)

Most of the necklines of coats and jackets that follow are the basic jewel shape. This is because the point of most coats and jackets is to keep you warm, so it's necessary to have the neckline close to your neck. However, you can still make a jacket with a V-neck to function more as a layering piece, or change it to a wide boatneck for a sixties look. For collars, you can add to the piece to make a big face-framing statement collar, or slim it down to make it barely noticeable. You can also not have a collar at all, which can look really chic—think of Michelle Obama's collarless, belted coats in pretty fabrics over pencil skirts. You can also play around with the collar point, making it pointier or more rounded. Don't be afraid to experiment!

SLEEVE LENGTHS AND SHAPES

The patterns included in this book have either set-in sleeves (constructed with shoulder seams and armholes) or raglan sleeves (a simpler, softer construction with a seam that goes from the underarm straight up to the neckline). While most jackets and coats have long sleeves, they don't always have to! Changing the sleeves' shape or adding cuffs can also result in a totally new look. Here are some sleeve options to familiarize yourself with.

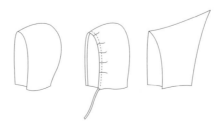

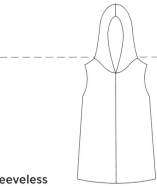

Sleeveless

Removing sleeves makes a coat or jacket into a vest—a great layer for seasonal transitions as well as a fun way to spice up an outfit in the warmer months (or indoors) à la Kate Moss.

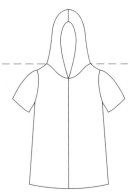

Short

This is a great, unexpected twist on a jacket. Rolled-up sleeves with epaulettes lend a touch of safari style, while short-sleeved wool coats look outrageously chic with opera-length gloves. It's not always the most practical option, but with the right layering, it will keep you feeling warm and looking cool.

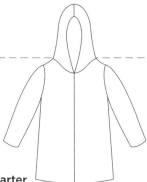

Three-Quarter

This sleeve length always screams Audrey Hepburn to me. It adds some chic to an evening coat. It can make a basic jacket a little edgier and more unexpected. It's also a stylish way to show off gloves, a hint of your long-sleeved top, or those cute, woolly arm warmers your best friend knitted for you.

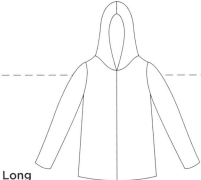

Long

Most jackets and coats have long sleeves, for obvious reasons—they keep you protected from the elements!

Bell

The bell shape looks very different depending on how long you make it: It can be a small flared ruffle (though probably not for the purposes of this book), a midlength angel sleeve, or a groovy, dramatically flared knuckle-duster (elegant for a black wool maxicoat).

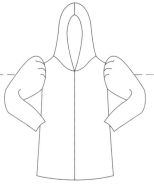

Puff

This is a versatile sleeve that can look retro cute or romantic, depending on the fabric and style of the jacket or coat.

DESIGNING WITH CUFFS

You don't always have to finish a sleeve with a separate piece, but it can add a bit of pizzazz to your design and serve a purpose, too (keeping your wrists warm). A simple shirt cuff as used in our jean jacket has a sporty look and can fold back or close with buttons; you can also play with size and shape. Other pieces and trims used to finish sleeves, like ruffles or elastic for a gathered closure, create a more feminine, dramatic flourish. You may also want to just go with a straightforward hemmed sleeve (for a clean look) or one designed to be rolled, or even prerolled and tacked in place (which conveys effortless cool).

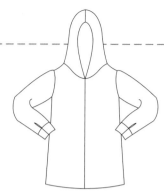

Shirt
This simple, classic closure is perfect for casual jackets and coats. You might also make it long and folded for a dramatic look, à la the French cuff of a dressy shirt.

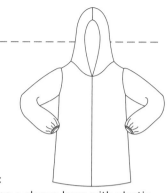

Elastic
Finishing a sleeve hem with elastic will gather the shape inward for a balloon look. Slashing and spreading the sleeve shape to make it more voluminous at the end will exaggerate this effect, if that's what you're after.

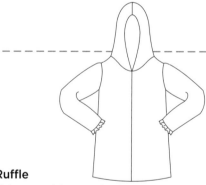

Ruffle
This can add a touch of sweetness to just about any sleeve: Try it with straight, not just gathered, sleeve endings.

Rolled
Slouchy and cool, this type of sleeve looks great with casual daytime looks (although you may want to tack it in place or add an epaulet to hold it up).

JACKET AND COAT LENGTHS

Don't think of the lengths the basic patterns come in—or even the individual project designs—as hard-and-fast rules. Hey, rules are meant to be broken! Almost any jacket or coat style in this book can be reinterpreted at almost any length, but it'll affect the function of the jacket (and the way you and your silhouette look), so plan carefully.

Above the Waist

Generally, this type of jacket would be considered a cropped or bolero jacket. It tends to be more about fashion than four-season function, but it makes a great layering piece to take the chill away on a summer night. The look is chic when fitted and slim over a billowy chiffon babydoll dress; you might also try making one that's boxy and cropped to wear with an oversized tee and cigarette jeans.

Waist

This versatile look is a great way to show off your waistline or a perfect-fitting pair of high-waisted pants.

Hip

Most jackets this length either hit midhip or cover your whole bum. This length works equally well for fitted and boxier styles.

Thigh

A midthigh-grazing hemline covers your hips and butt while leaving your legs (and the bottom of your dress) on display, which is why many women favor it. This length is ideal for casual day coats or longer parka-style jackets.

Knee

This versatile length is practical for day or evening. It fully covers up knee-length and shorter dresses—a good thing to consider if it's raining or cold! Knee-length coats also look wonderful with knee-high boots, although some petite women find them unflattering.

Full

Midcalf or ankle-length hems are dramatic and chic—and they'll keep you warmer than all other coats in winter. Perfect for evening (it'll cover a long gown and make an elegant statement), this type of coat can also be made casual in a woolly fabric for pairing with jeans and boots.

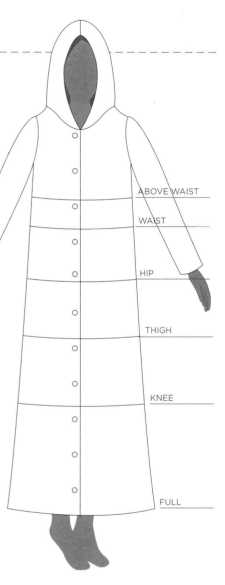

ABOVE WAIST

WAIST

HIP

THIGH

KNEE

FULL

LENDING A HAND: POCKETS

Pockets serve an important function—a place to put your hands and your stuff—and can really make a difference in the look of a coat or jacket, especially in the case of patch pockets, which are visible on the outside of the garment. They can evoke work wear (rectangular flap pockets closed with snaps) or add a vintage twist (heart-shaped pockets, anyone?), so don't be afraid to play around with them to make an unexpected statement on your chosen silhouette. Then again, you may prefer a cleaner look, in which case side-seam pockets do the trick. Going pocketless is an option too, albeit one that works best for layering pieces (a cropped bolero, for instance) rather than outerwear meant for out-of-doors. I love kangaroo pockets—they keep your hands warm and look sporty. It's fun to add a kangeroo pocket on a nonsporty piece like a wool tweed pullover for a surprise sporty twist.

Kangaroo Pocket

This type of pocket is sewn on top of the garment as well and mimics a kangaroo pouch. It keeps your hands warm. Feel free to play with the proportions and angles of openings.

Patch Pockets

This type of pocket is sewn on top of the garment. It's often used for fitted jackets that don't leave room for you to put your hands inside. You can change its shape and entry point—either at the top or side—and add flaps. Don't be afraid to think outside the rectangle! You can also add gathering or pleats to a patch pocket to create more room, as well as visual interest.

Side Seam or Inseam Pockets

These pockets are inside of the coat, hidden in the side seam. The style works best for loose-fitting jackets and coats, so that you won't have to wriggle to get your hands inside. If you don't want the look of pockets ruining the line, this option is for you.

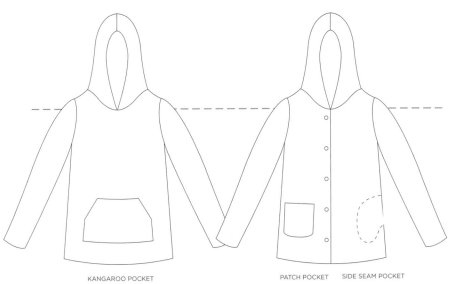

KANGAROO POCKET

PATCH POCKET   SIDE SEAM POCKET

COAT AND JACKET CLOSURES

Generally, the opening of a coat or jacket is at the center front. For the purposes of this book we are going to stick with that, but if you decide you want to get more creative with your coats and jackets, feel free to use this same information if opening the coat or jacket from the back, the shoulder, or the side seam. Coats and jackets either close by meeting at the center front *kissing*, or one falls on top of the other with the help of a front *extension*.

Kissing Front

With a kissing front, the two sides are symmetrical, meaning that whatever connects them is visible. There are several choices for connecting a kissing front. You can use a zipper, toggles, frog closures (Asian-style corded closures that resemble their namesake), or ties. For certain styles, you may want nothing at all except for a tiny hidden hook and eye to make it look like more like a cover-up than a functioning jacket (this is most likely to come in handy for evening looks and fun, not functional, pieces).

Extension Closures

Most coats and jackets have an overlapping extension closure, buttons and buttonholes being the most common. Snaps also require an extension closure, and zippers can be done this way too—they'll be covered by a flap, which is helpful on, say, a winter coat so that you won't have a frozen metal zipper exposed to the cold. Generally speaking, extension closures are warmer than kissing closures, since the opening is covered by an overlap of fabric that blocks the wind and precipitation.

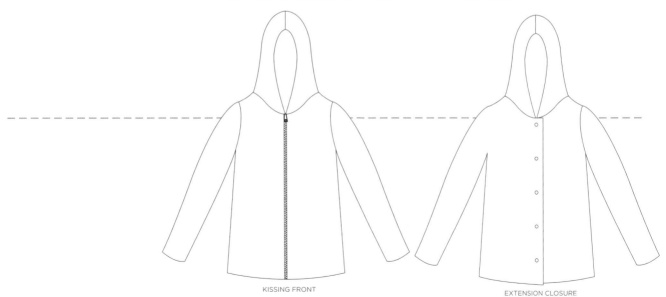

KISSING FRONT

EXTENSION CLOSURE

material world
CHOOSING FABRICS

Shopping for fabrics and trims is always the most fun and inspiring part of designing. Some are easier to work with than others: When I first started sewing, I always made my coats out of basic cotton canvas because it was easy to use and cheap; it worked great for army jackets and jean styles. As I grew up, I could afford investing in fancy double-faced cashmere coating and worsted-wool suiting fabric from Italy, and I branched into dressier looks with linings.

If a fabric you love seems a bit too fragile for a jacket or coat, you don't have to give up on it: You can create a more substantial fabric by ironing interfacing on the entire body of fabric to make it stiffer and thicker in feel. Sometimes I will fuse the entire length of fabric with interfacing before cutting when it's feeling kind of flimsy. Lining a coat also makes it more substantial and winter friendly; it can also make wools and other napped and textured fabrics much easier to slip in and out of. Here's a list of fabrics that work well with the different coat and jacket projects in this book.

COATED

Many fabrics, from cotton to wool, are treated with a water-repellent coating on either the face or the inside, which is great for activewear and rainwear. It may be visible (like a layer of PVC or wax) or invisible (a chemical treatment), but if you've bought one, be ultra careful when ironing it, because you don't want to melt your new creation! Try a test swatch first, keep the iron on low, and use a layer in between the fabric and the iron. Ask the person at your fabric store for advice about how to press and care for the specific fabric you've chosen.

COTTON

Classic, crisp, and usually casual, cotton is pretty breathable, which is why it works best for spring and summer coats and jackets. Of course, there are ways to break that rule; you could pair a heavy cotton twill with a wool-blanket lining and fare just fine in the cold November rain.

Corduroy

This snuggly napped fabric, available in a variety of weights, is not just great for scholarly chic fall jackets and coats—it also makes a fun textural detail, like a collar or cuff, on a jacket in a different fabric.

Denim

This wardrobe mainstay is available in different weights, so you can adapt it for any time of year. Just be sure to wash the fabric first. You can have fun with bleaching it, too! A denim jacket or vest is a great project you'll wear all the time. Line yours with plaid flannel or fuzzy fleece to take you through the chillier months.

Piqué

This finely textured fabric is thicker and stiffer than ordinary cotton—perfect for preppy summer jackets,

but it could also be cool for a chic fall trench.

Quilted

Colorful quilted cotton prints can be found at most sewing stores. They're soft, cozy, and not as heavy as they might sound. Because they are reversible, they are ideal for simple all-season jackets with bias-bound edges for that boho look.

Terry Cloth

The interlocking cotton loops make this absorbent fabric ideal for summer cover-ups and activewear. What could be cuter than a terry track jacket?

Twill and Canvas

These basic, workmanlike weaves come in light and heavyweight varieties, and are great for day jackets like army or golf-style jackets.

LEATHER AND LEATHERETTE

For biker looks, nothing is better than leather—just keep in mind that it's expensive and hard to sew, requiring a special leather needle and sometimes even a special machine (ask your fabric

salesperson). Leather also comes in skins, not yardage, so you may have to patch things together in smaller segments than the patterns call for (which can, of course, look really cool). Faux leather and suede are more affordable options, and they're sold on the roll rather than by the hide, making the cutting process easier to figure out. They're synthetic and scorch easily, so iron with caution!

LINEN

This natural, ultrabreathable fabric is great for airy spring jackets and coats. It has an easy, bohemian charm that lends itself well to embellishment and embroidery.

NYLON

This synthetic fabric is useful for activewear and looser shapes of jackets and coats, as well as the exterior of parkas. Try making a matching pouch to roll a nylon rain jacket into!

PILE FABRICS

Fabrics in this family, such as faux fur and velvet, have a raised surface. Be careful when you cut, because not only are they *one-way fabrics*—meaning the nap of the fabric looks different from different angles, so the pieces must be laid out in one direction—but it also leaves tons of little hairs all over the place after you cut. Smaller piles such as velvet work great as jackets. Shaggier piles, like faux fur, are best when used as details like cuffs or collars, or in small garments like cropped jackets. But hey, don't be afraid to rock a full-length faux-fur coat in the winter, if that's your style!

SILK

This is a strong, beautiful, and breathable—albeit usually pricey—fabric made in different weights and styles. I suggest silk twills, shantungs, twill-back satin, and blends with wool for dressy jackets and coats. Stay away from flimsy charmeuses.

WOOL

The most popular fiber for coating fabrics, wool runs the gamut from warm and fuzzy to crisp, smooth, and professional.

Boiled

This thick, warm wool has a bit of a nubby feel. It also has a bit of stretchiness to it. You know how you sometimes put your favorite sweater in the washing machine by accident and it gets shrunk and dense? That's kind of what boiled wool is like. You can use it in the same way as double-faced wool (just don't throw your new coat in the washing machine): It's usually left unlined (and therefore a good place to play with contrast binding).

Bouclé

This nubby wool, sometimes woven with multicolored yarns, is an interesting midweight fabric for dressy jackets and coats with wonderful texture. Think Chanel, and you've got the picture.

Cashmere

This luxury fabric makes any coat look top-notch. It costs a lot, but it looks and feels like it!

Double-Faced

Both sides of double-faced wool can be used as the face of a jacket or coat. Available in a range of weights and interesting textures, it's ideal for unlined coats; try finishing the raw edges with a decorative binding so that you can show off the inside as well as the outside.

Felt

Usually thick and stiff, felt—which is actually made by mashing, not weaving, the fibers—is great for structured shapes.

Herringbone

A two-tone patterned fabric with a scholarly menswear vibe that's fun for fall. Try contrasting it with leather trim.

Suiting

This smooth, elegant wool weave is best for jackets either in classic menswear-inspired looks or with strong tailoring. You can also sex it up a bit with fun trims and contrast lining in a bright color or animal print.

Tweed

This two-tone nubby fabric is fantastic for fall jackets, and in its heavier incarnations it works for winter coats, too. I highly recommend lining it to prevent itching and shedding.

THE INSIDE SCOOP: *LININGS*

Linings create a smooth surface that lets you slide into your jacket or coat. They're most important when the coat or jacket fabric is "sticky" or high friction, like wool. Sometimes you can get away with just lining the sleeves for smoothness, but if you want to make a better quality coat, then I'd say to fully line it. If warmth is a concern, lining also makes a lot of sense; you can also line the body of a winter coat with thin fuzzy fleece (but it's not recommended for sleeves, since you'll have trouble getting into them if you're wearing a thick sweater).

For some wool fabrics, like boiled wool or double-faced wool, it's better not to line them, since those wools are smooth and easy to slip into; plus you want to show off how nice the fabric is. For casual fabrics like cotton canvas, you don't need lining unless you want it for style (like lining a cotton golf jacket with a madras plaid). In fact, you can line anything you want for added flair. Sometime I line the body of a jacket with a fun fabric, like striped cotton, and then line the sleeves with lining fabric so that it's smooth but not visible.

Acetate Taffeta

This slippery synthetic is the most basic lining fabric, and it's available in tons of colors at a good price.

China Silk

Very lightweight, this is to be used with equally lightweight fabrics like silk twill. Expensive but worth it if you want a luxurious keepsake!

Flannel-Back Satin

You can have the best of both worlds—this lining has a smooth satin face with a flannel back that goes inside, perfect for adding extra warmth to a coat.

Twill

A twill weave gives a more luxurious, textured look to coat linings. Just make sure it's not too "frictiony" to slip into.

SUPPORT SYSTEM: *INTERFACINGS*

These synthetic support fabrics are essential for adding weight and durability to pieces on a garment where there is heavy usage, like areas that have closures such as buttonhole extensions, cuff, collars, facings and pocket flaps. Sometimes, as I mentioned earlier in this chapter, if I am using a flimsy fabric and want to stiffen it up a bit, I will use interfacing throughout the whole garment. Interfacings are available in different weights; depending on the weight of the fabric and how much heft you want to add, try testing out a few varieties on a swatch of your fabric first. They come in the *fusible* variety, which is ironed onto the wrong side of the fabric, or the *sew-in* kind, which is basted on at the seam allowances. Mostly I use fusible, unless the fabric I am using is too synthetic and too melt-prone to iron, in which case I will use sew-in interfacing.

extra credit

TRIMS TO TRY

The smallest bells and whistles can make a huge difference in the style of a coat or jacket. I always make an effort to spice up the details in the outerwear for my own collection, whether it's fun anchor buttons on a peacoat or streamlined leather piping on a dramatic swing-shaped coat. Why not play around with some of these yourself? Hit the fabric store— or even an antiques market—to check out buttons, zippers, tassels, and toggles. The smallest detail could spark an idea for a whole new coat!

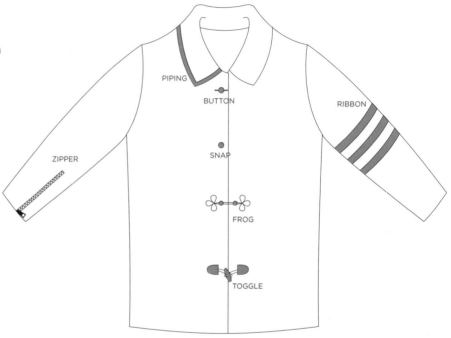

PIPING

This tape, which is sewn inside seams and has a tubular decorative cord that stays on the outside, is great for outlining curves and showing off seaming details. I like inserting it into collars and pocket edges.

RIBBONS

I topstitch ribbon onto cuffs, collars, and front plackets to add a fun touch without too much work. Try using contrast ribbon around pocket edges or striped ribbon on the epaulets of an army jacket.

CLOSURES

Jackets and coats don't have to have closures—certain styles, such as floral-print quilted shell jackets, look effortless and fresh as slip-on jackets. However, zippers, buttons, toggles, snaps, and the like perform an important function, especially on cold-weather outerwear. Each type of closure also evokes a particular style vibe: Snaps look utilitarian; toggles look woodsy and cute; zippers can look punky or athletic, depending on which type you use. This is really a place to get creative, so feel free to switch up my suggestions for the individual projects. Look for oversized or contrast-color closures, or try substituting a closure most often used on a different type of jacket (say, rugged metal hardware on a classic peacoat).

Buttons

These can be functional or purely decorative, and come in a variety of sizes, styles, and colors. They're really fun to use as a design detail—even if you change nothing else about a basic project, you can easily change these! Oversized buttons can turn a simple navy peacoat into a fresh, mod statement piece, while vintage military buttons take an army jacket to the next level. Use your imagination, and don't just go for what matches; buttons in fun shapes and contrasting colors can give any coat or jacket an extra dose of personality.

Snaps

Great to use if you want to hide a closure or as a button alternative, snaps come in many sizes and colors and can add their own industrial charm to a garment. I love to use them on little fitted cotton jackets. Most fabric stores sell snap guns to easily attach snaps to garments. It can get a bit tricky with thicker fabrics, though, so for those try the sew-in snaps that you just tack on with a bit of thread.

Toggles and Frogs

Bold and functional, toggles have a timeless, collegiate appeal that's great for *Love Story*-esque wool coats. Frog closures resemble the animal they're named after and are traditionally a part of Asian dress; they add elegance to fancy silky jackets.

Zippers

Separating zippers are available with coiled or teeth edges in metal or plastic and in different sizes. I'm partial to medium-sized separating brass zippers—they have a classic look to them that I love. But a small-toothed plastic zipper looks great on, say, a nylon track jacket. Don't be afraid to draw attention to zippers as design details—try leaving a contrasting color of zipper tape exposed, or using chunky silver zippers to add a touch of biker-girl toughness.

CONSIDERING FABRIC WEIGHT AND DRAPE

Fabric weight and drape is a design element, too, and an oft-overlooked opportunity to get creative. With coats and jackets, it's especially important because it often means the difference between, well, a coat and a jacket! (For example, a bomber shape could be made in faux fur for winter and lightweight cotton twill for summer, using the very same pattern.) Where and when you'll be wearing your outerwear will obviously influence the fabric you use. Don't be afraid to get creative and make a classic shape in a totally unexpected fabric weight; it's a great way to keep your look fresh and different, and this is how designers often think. A sporty track jacket silhouette in warm wool? Why not?

Weight is also something you need to take into account when deciding on closures and other trims. Delicate snaps may not stay snapped if you use them with heavyweight wool; big toggles might suit the fabric better. On the other end of things, a chunky #10 metal zipper will overwhelm a featherweight nylon windbreaker. It may eat up the fabric when you zip and unzip, and it will almost certainly sag down the front, creating bubbly bulges around your stomach—probably not the look you're after.

CHAPTER 2

PATTERN PLAY

USING THEM, ALTERING THEM, KEEPING THEM IN SHAPE

BEHIND EVERY GREAT JACKET OR COAT IS A GREAT PATTERN—
the building blocks of a garment as translated onto paper. This book, as I've mentioned, includes three basic patterns that I rely on every season as the basis for outerwear in my own collection—the fitted jacket (which has princess seams), the basic jacket, and the straight coat (which has raglan sleeves). Each has a unique construction that can form the basis for a wide array of silhouettes, whether it's a shrunken bolero or a dramatic maxicoat. They're time-tested templates for the design projects offered later in the book—and infinitely customizable for your own genius designs.

Why reacquaint yourself with patterns now? While making a garment without a pattern is bound to cause problems, making a coat or jacket without a pattern is impossible. Outerwear is often comprised of many special components—extensions, facings, collars—that require some special attention to get right. Even if you're a regular home sewer, give this chapter a read: It's always useful to refamiliarize yourself with the structure of how garments come together, especially as it pertains to coats and jackets.

This book will also get into some light patternmaking—for our purposes, this will refer to the process of altering the shape of the three basic patterns to actualize your designs. You'll do this first to get the fit right, and again each time you create a new project. Some designers have a clear vision of the silhouette of a garment first, while others get the initial spark of their ideas from fabric or trims. Whichever way you get inspired, you'll need to understand the properties of each of the three basic jacket patterns included in the book first. I'll show you how to choose your size—and how to customize each pattern's fit within that size so that every project in this book works flawlessly with your figure. Once you have all that down pat, you can really get creative, altering the details to create a one-of-a-kind jacket or coat that fits you—and your style—perfectly.

Patterns are delicate and contain a lot of important information, so this chapter will also include some pointers about how to transfer each pattern to regular paper and get it ready for fabric cutting, a process designers call "trueing the pattern."

tools of the trade

PATTERNMAKING AND CUTTING SUPPLIES

No pattern whiz gets to work without these essentials on hand. Keep these items in a bin near your worktable so that they're easy to grab and hard to lose!

Paper scissors: Your basic pair from an office-supply store will work great.

Fabric scissors: Make sure yours are strong and sharp, especially if you are working with a thick wool fabric. Don't use them on paper or anything that isn't fabric!

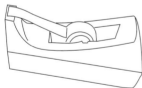

Clear tape: Regular magic tape is fine.

Roll of paper: I buy wide (at least 30" or 76cm) banner paper from an art supply store.

Measuring tape: The laminated yellow fabric type works for me. A stiff metal construction tape measure will not!

Pencil: #2: Make sure it's sharp.

18" (45.5cm) clear ruler: This is the most important tool for patternmaking. It's available at most art supply stores.

Weights: You can buy special weights at your local fabric store to hold down fabric and paper pattern pieces on the worktable, or just try using some soup cans from your cupboard.

Pins: Pins are handy for keeping little corners of patterns in place (even if you are primarily using weights). Just make sure to pin them through the seam allowance to avoid pinholes in the body of your garment.

Tracing wheel: With its little spiky wheel, this tool (sold at sewing shops) is essential for transferring patterns.

French curve: This tool has an array of different-shaped curves that you can trace for armholes and necklines.

Awl: This sharp tool is perfect for marking holes in patterns, but you can also use a small nail and hammer it through with one of your weights in hand.

Washable marker or chalk: Buy these specialty items at your local sewing store. It's important that the mark can be washed or brushed off, so test it first—you don't want to stain your precious fabric.

the three amigos

GETTING TO KNOW YOUR PATTERNS

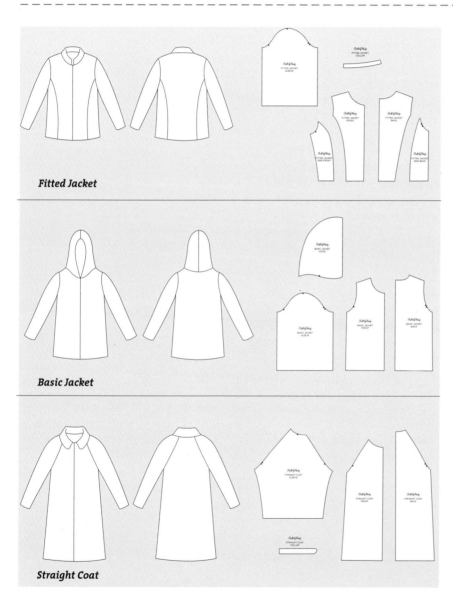

Fitted Jacket

Basic Jacket

Straight Coat

There are three basic patterns included in this book. Before you tear open the package, acquaint yourself with their various components so you'll know what to do with them! I also suggest first scanning through the project chapters for a sense of how you'll change them up and give them your own personal spin. Once the packet is open, you'll have to preserve them carefully, so don't be in a hurry!

SIZING YOURSELF UP

To determine which size you'll wear in the patterns provided in this book, use a soft tape measure (not Dad's stiff metal hardware version) on four specific places: the shoulders, bust, waist, and hips. While serious professionals often take more measurements than that, for the purposes of this book, it will suffice (especially since I'll teach you how to tweak the basic fit in this chapter). If possible, enlist a friend to make sure the tape is straight—better safe than sorry!

size wise

WHERE DO YOU FIT IN?

You may find that your measurements correspond to one size on top and a different size on the bottom—in fact, it's highly likely! What to do? Well, if we were making shirts, the most important measurement is your bust and shoulders; for skirts and pants, it's the waist and hip measurements. Coats longer than waist length, however, have to fit you in both places. If your upper and lower body areas are drastically different in size, choose the size that fits your bust best, then for longer coats add or subtract width to the lower half of the jacket or coat (which is way easier to work with than the top half). Later I will show you how to make changes to your basic patterns so that each design project fits like a glove.

Shoulders
Measure straight across between the point where your clavicle bone ends near each arm.

Bust
Measure around the fullest part of your bust.

Waist
Measure your natural waist—the smallest part of your waist. You might want to use a mirror and tie a string around your waist first to find the most accurate point.

Hip
Measure the fullest part of your hip—usually about 7" to 9" (18cm to 23cm) below your natural waistline.

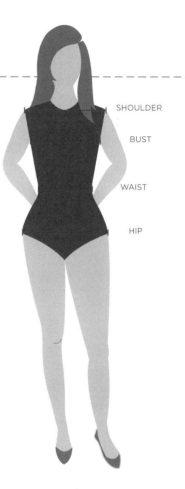

SHOULDER

BUST

WAIST

HIP

MEASUREMENT CHART

	XS	Small	Medium	Large	XL
Shoulder	13" (33cm)	13½" (34.5cm)	14" (35.5cm)	14½" (37cm)	15" (38cm)
Bust	32"–33" (81cm–84cm)	34"–35" (86cm–89cm)	36"–37" (91cm–94cm)	38"–39" (96.5cm–99cm)	40"–41" (101.5cm–104cm)
Waist	25"–26" (63.5cm–66cm)	27"–28" (69cm–71cm)	29"–30" (74cm–76cm)	31"–32" (79cm–81cm)	33"–34" (84cm–86cm)
Hip	35"–36" (89cm–91cm)	37"–38" (94cm–96.5cm)	39"–40" (99cm–101.5cm)	41"–42" (104cm–106.5cm)	43"–44" (109cm–112cm)

open source
UNPACKING THE PATTERNS

Now that you know what to expect, it's safe to gently remove the folded patterns from the envelope. These patterns are placed in what's called a nested layout: The sizes are placed on top of each other on the same sheet. With your iron on low, carefully press out the folds of each piece of paper and cut the areas for each of the pattern pieces apart. Stack all of the pieces for each style together, and store them this way before you even think about leaving the room—otherwise (trust me), a hood or sleeve piece is all too likely to drift into your paper recycling bin.

Built by Wendy
BASIC JACKET
SLEEVE

DOTS AND SLASHES: *THE MEANINGS OF MARKINGS*

Before you can test out the patterns to make sure they fit properly, it's important to know what the different pattern markings mean.

Notches

These small tapered slits function as placement instructions. In this book, notches appear on the slopers (basic patterns), but you'll have to transfer each notch to the same position on the outer edge of the seam allowance once you add it. Notches can indicate many things:

- They can appear in corresponding places to indicate which seams are to be sewn together.
- They mark where the legs of a dart begin.
- They mark gathering points, such as the point where the two folds of a pleat meet.
- They distinguish between front and back pieces: Usually, a double notch (two notches placed ¼" to ½", or 6mm to 13mm, apart) signifies the back piece. So on a coat bodice, for instance, there will be a single notch marking the armhole for the front piece and a double notch marking the armhole on the back piece. Then, on the sleeve cap piece, which is sewn to both the front and back armholes, you'll find both single and double notches. Simply line up each type of notch, and you'll know where to sew the pieces together.

Grain lines

These arrows point in one direction or another. The grain line should run parallel to the fabric's selvage edge.

NOTCH

Built by Wendy
BASIC JACKET
FRONT

GRAINLINE

copy right
TRANSFERRING PATTERNS TO NEW PAPER

Once you've settled on a size, the smart thing to do is to immediately trace the original pattern piece in your size from the nest onto new, sturdier paper and store the tissue version away. Why the rush? You only get one set of patterns with your book—they need to be protected! Tissue paper simply isn't designed to withstand cutting;

it's only designed to be light and compact. You'll still need to test the pattern's fit to make sure it works for your body, so you'll need a version that can be cut with fabric. Also, if for some reason the size you picked isn't correct, you can refer back to the original nested layout and pick your correct size.

1. Place the original pressed pattern sheet on top of a piece of paper (white kraft paper is good, but you can also tape together pieces of printer paper in a pinch).

2. Using your tracing wheel, move along the lines that correspond to your size.

3. Remove the original pattern, and look closely at your paper. You will see tiny little dots.

4. Take your pencil and trace lightly over the dots. Work with your clear ruler and French curve to smooth any jagged lines.

5. Label each piece with its correct name and size, such as "Straight Coat, Sleeve, Size M."

6. Stop—DO NOT CUT THE PIECES OUT YET! Read on to see what you'll do next with the pattern.

TIP:
You might want to place some poster board or a self-healing mat (available at art and sewing stores) beneath your paper and patterns so that your tracing wheel spikes don't mark up your mom's fancy dining-room table.

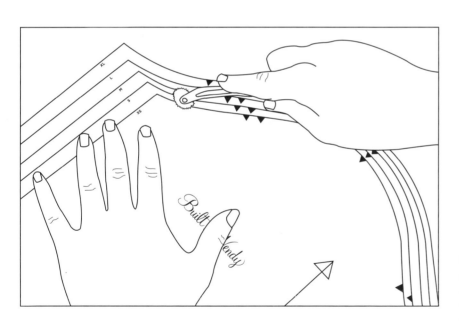

fit club
PUTTING YOUR PATTERNS TO THE TEST

LIVING ON THE EDGE: *UNDERSTANDING THE SEAM ALLOWANCE*

Heads-Up: The patterns in this book do NOT have seam allowances!

Why? This makes it simpler to cut them apart and play around with them without having to sort out where the allowances are and where they've been cut off. For coats, which can get complicated, it's a better place to start—trust me. (Basic patterns without seam allowances used for the purpose of patternmaking are sometimes called slopers.)

What does this mean? Before you cut fabric for the projects in this book, you'll have to add a seam allowance along the pattern pieces to allow for the portion of the seam that is inside the garment. I'll remind you about this step for each project later in the book, but it should be committed to memory, especially if you plan to create your own projects using the basic patterns. I think ⅝" (16mm) seam allowances—which many store-bought patterns have—are too big, especially around curved seams, where they tend to get bunchy. Seams can be trimmed down after sewing, but it's easier to do things the right way first. I prefer to add ½" (13mm) allowance on most seams, and ¼" (6mm) around small, curved areas like necklines.

In the patternmaking sections of each project, please refer to this color-coded chart—it will indicate which size seam allowance to add for each seam. Just don't forget to add them!

Purple= ¼" (6mm)

Orange= ½" (13mm)

■ ¼"

■ ½"

After measuring yourself and transferring the correct pattern size to sturdier paper, it's still a good idea to test the fit of each of the three patterns first before you go whip up five pricey cashmere coats, only to discover that your large bust is busting out! Women's bodies come in every shape and proportion, and because coats and jackets are meant to actually cover them, this step is particularly important for the basic patterns in this book. A muslin is a test garment—in the industry, they're made of inexpensive cotton muslin, hence the name—that allows designers to calibrate a garment's fit without letting the real fabric go to waste.

1. Add the seam allowances to the pattern pieces you traced earlier in step 4 (don't bother with hems and necklines, as you won't need to finish them on the muslin, and therefore they'll fall in the same place as on the finished garment).

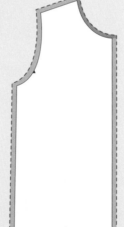

altered state

TIPS FOR FIXING FIT

2. Cut out the patterns.

3. Place the patterns onto the muslin fabric (if you don't have actual muslin, use leftover fabric or something inexpensive) and cut out each piece.

4. Stitch or pin the pattern pieces together. Don't bother finishing the seam allowances, since you won't be wearing this jacket anywhere (at least I hope not).

5. Try on the muslin and note where anything is too tight, too loose, too long, or too short so that you can adjust the basic patterns accordingly. Keep in mind whether you plan to wear heavy sweaters underneath the coat, or whether, say, you'll be sewing in a thick, padded down lining that will make the coat feel more snug.

The patterns in this book are based on real Built by Wendy patterns that are, in my experience, flattering to most people. But because of the incredible diversity of the human race and especially the female species, no pattern can fit absolutely everyone absolutely everywhere. Once you make your muslin, note if it's too tight, too loose, too short, too long, or proportionally off. What to do? Don't despair, repair! Here are some ideas for how to alter the basic pattern.

TOO TIGHT

1. Leaving the coat open, measure the distance that the fabric spreads apart at the bust.

2. Divide that measurement by four, add that amount to each side seam from the armhole, and blend a new seam line down to the bottom opening.

3. Add that same measurement to the sleeve side seams too, and blend these lines.

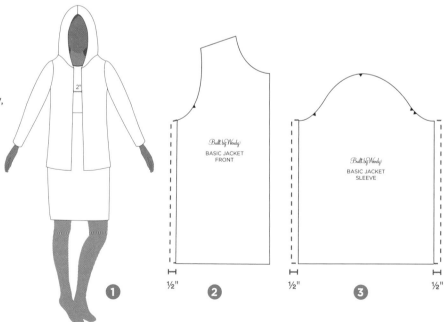

altered state CONTINUED

TOO LOOSE

1. Remove the sleeves and turn the coat inside out.

2. Pin the coat along the side seams where you want to tighten the fit.

3. Measure from the seam line to the new pin marks, and remove that amount from your pattern, including the sleeves.

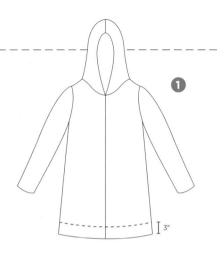

TOO LONG

1. Pin the sleeves or the hem to the correct length. Have a friend help you if you're shortening a hem, if possible. Otherwise, mark the spot with chalk and take the coat off to pin it, then try it on again to be sure.

2. Subtract that amount from the basic pattern, and shorten or fold the pattern piece to make a new version.

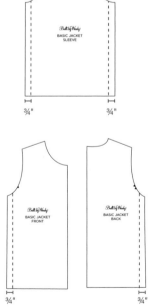

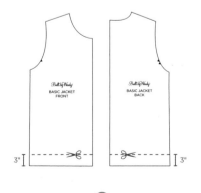

TOO SHORT

1. Measure from the coat's edge to the ideal position where you would like the sleeve or hem to end. This is much easier to do with someone helping you!

2. Add that amount to the basic pattern using simple addition or slashing and spreading. (See box on following page for more explanation on that.)

PROPORTION IS OFF

If, for instance, you're tall and long-waisted and the waistline of the coat hits your rib cage, or you're petite and the bust hits too low, measure the distance that the waist and bust are off, and use a slash-and-spread or folding technique to ensure that the waist and bust land in the correct position for your body. In this case, simply adding and subtracting to the pattern edge isn't a good idea, because that will change the shape, but not the proportion, of the style.

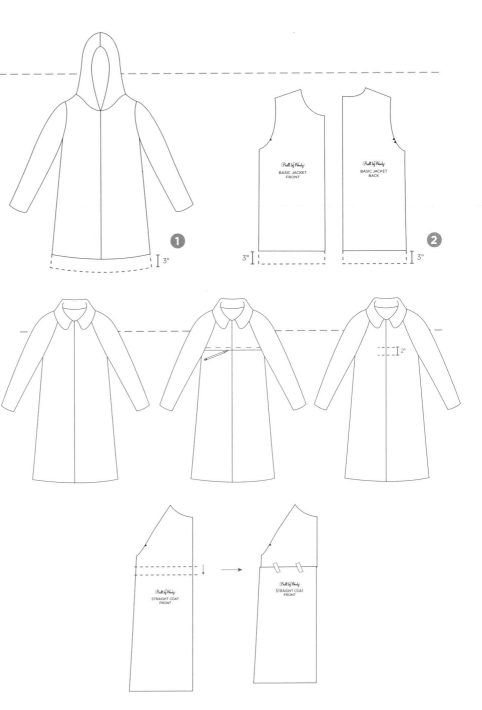

SHAPE SHIFTERS: *BASIC PATTERNMAKING TECHNIQUES*

Adding

To make a garment wider or longer, you can either add to the seams or you can use the slash-and-spread method. Let's say you want to add 2" (5cm) to the length of your dress. You can simply use your ruler to trace the hem line 2" (5cm) below where it was onto a new piece of paper (use tape or a weight to hold the sloper down) and then extend the seam lines downward with your pencil, taping the new piece to the old.

Or, to use the *slash-and-spread* technique, make a slash line within the pattern, cut across the line, and spread the pattern pieces 2" (5cm) apart on top of more paper. Then, tape them down and connect the pieces with pencil lines along the side seams. If you want to make a skirt or bodice or sleeve wider, the same techniques apply.

What's the difference? Slashing and spreading keeps the outer seams of the pattern piece intact, so it's a wise choice if you want to keep a garment's proportion exactly the same.

Subtracting

Similarly, you can make your dress length shorter by simply cutting off 2" (5cm) across the hem. Or, you can use a technique called folding where you draw a line within the pattern then another line 2" (5cm) above it and fold the pattern so the lines are together. The same goes for making a skirt or bodice narrower, a sleeve shorter, and so on. Folding will preserve the proportion of the piece more precisely; it's up to you which technique you prefer to use. A sleeve or hem with a distinct flared or tapered shape, for instance, might lose its impact if you simply chop it off; folding will remove the length or width from within the body rather than along the edge, again keeping the exact shape the same. Then again, a straight coat is a straight coat, and if you only need to lose an inch or two (2.5cm to 5cm), simply cutting off that length will save time.

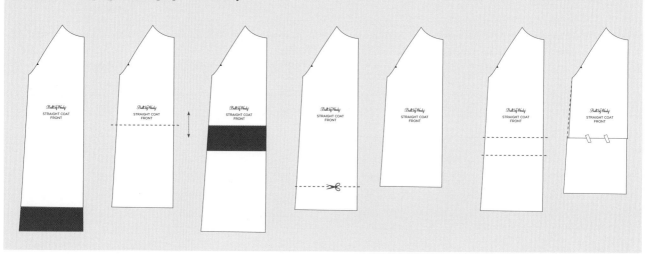

permanent record

FINALIZING PATTERNS

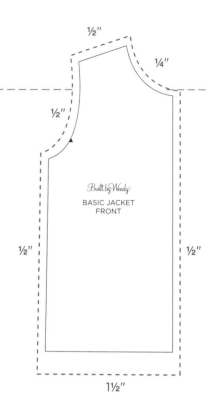

½"

¼"

½"

Built by Wendy
BASIC JACKET
FRONT

½"

½"

1½"

CORE VALUES: MAKING A SLOPER SET

Once you have made changes to your pattern, transfer it (again!) to a fresh sheet of paper by tracing around the edges using your pencil. Now you have created your sloper set, a perfect-fitting template that will form the basis for every jacket you make. You can also transfer these onto poster board so they last longer (which I highly recommend). Then each time you begin a new project, simply trace around the sloper pieces, make your alterations, and then true your pattern (see the next step).

ON YOUR MARK: TRUEING THE PATTERN

To true (create final markings for) your pattern, draw the seam allowances by using your clear ruler to mark points along the outside of the pattern at the appropriate width from pattern's edge, and connect the points, following the shape of the pattern. Use your tracing wheel to transfer the grain lines and other markings to the new pattern piece. Label and cut out each piece. Now, your pattern is ready to be laid onto fabric for cutting and sewing. Consult the instructions for each design project for specific trueing information.

THE BOTTOM LINE: *HEMS*

How to hem a coat or jacket really depends on the style and weight of the fabric. Generally, more equals more. A wider hem on a heavy coat makes it look a lot nicer than a thin hem, and it makes functional sense, too: For instance, on a thick, long wool coat, a 2" (5cm) hem will be easier to work with and allow the coat to hang nicely, whereas on a thinner wool jacket you might want only a 1" (2.5cm)

hem so that you don't have all that folded-in bulk weighting you down. On a light canvas jacket, something smaller, like ½" (13mm), should suffice. For each of the projects in this book, I will note the hem size, and the seam allowance you'll need to add for the hem. If you design your own creation, remember to add it!

Seam Allowances for Hems

For all hems larger than 1" (2.5cm) add a ½" (13mm) seam allowance. For all hems

shorter than 1" (2.5cm), add a ¼" (6mm) seam allowance.

Seam Allowance Finishings

When you add a hem to the opening of a garment (such as the sleeve opening or bottom opening), that area is folded back and not joined to another piece, but you still need to add a seam allowance to the hem for the finishing process. Otherwise your sleeve (or entire coat) will be a bit too short!

bits and pieces

PATTERNMAKING FOR SMALLER ELEMENTS

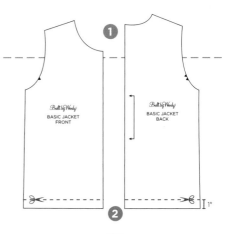

FACINGS AND LININGS

In each of the sewing projects in this book, I'll teach you how to make patterns for the different pieces you need—but there are some common pieces that are used over and over. Knowing about these pieces and the techniques for altering them will give you the skills to expand on the projects yourself. For instance, if you want to line a coat that we are showing unlined, here's where you'll learn the skills to make a lining. So read on, and read carefully!

Facings

Facings are mirror-image inside pieces whose purpose is to finish seams around openings, such as neck openings. You can make a facing in any width you want, but generally they are about 2" to 3" (5cm to 7.5cm) wide.

1. Trace your sloper onto a fresh piece of paper.

2. Using your clear ruler, trace 2" (5cm) in from the edge, following the shape of the edge.

3. Add the seam allowances.

Linings

When making a pattern for lining a garment, you'll basically mirror the entire garment, minus 1" (2.5cm) from the bottom and sleeve openings.

1. Trace the entire sloper onto a fresh piece of paper.

2. Remove 1" (2.5cm) from the bottom and sleeve openings.

3. Add the seam allowances and hems.

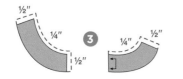

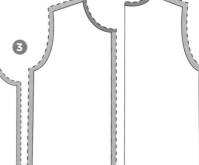

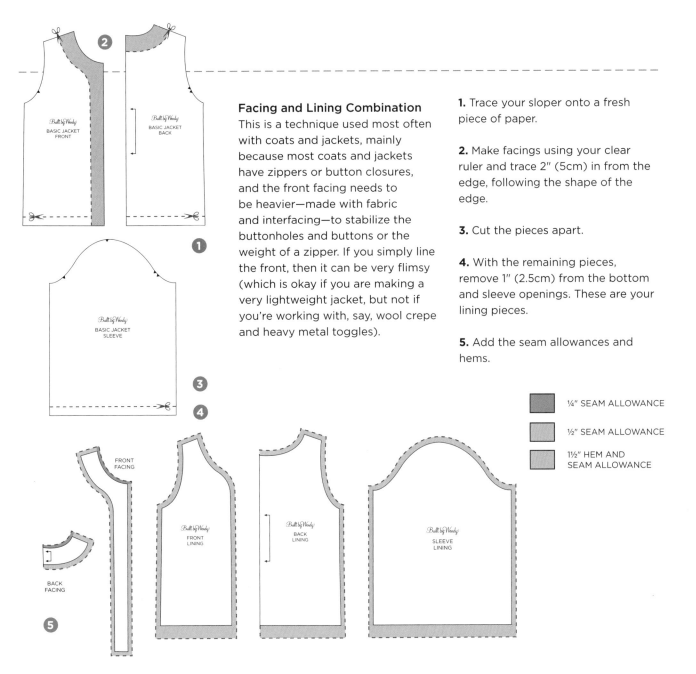

Facing and Lining Combination

This is a technique used most often with coats and jackets, mainly because most coats and jackets have zippers or button closures, and the front facing needs to be heavier—made with fabric and interfacing—to stabilize the buttonholes and buttons or the weight of a zipper. If you simply line the front, then it can be very flimsy (which is okay if you are making a very lightweight jacket, but not if you're working with, say, wool crepe and heavy metal toggles).

1. Trace your sloper onto a fresh piece of paper.

2. Make facings using your clear ruler and trace 2″ (5cm) in from the edge, following the shape of the edge.

3. Cut the pieces apart.

4. With the remaining pieces, remove 1″ (2.5cm) from the bottom and sleeve openings. These are your lining pieces.

5. Add the seam allowances and hems.

¼″ SEAM ALLOWANCE

½″ SEAM ALLOWANCE

1½″ HEM AND SEAM ALLOWANCE

FRONT EXTENSIONS

Most coats and jackets have front extensions, since they are most likely closed with a button or snap front. Even zippers usually need some sort of extension piece to function at their best. I'll explain how to make the proper extension for each of the design projects, but it's a smart bet to familiarize yourself with how they work first.

Button Extension

Unlike zippers, which can zip straight up the center of a jacket, a buttoned front needs an extension to create space for the button. The width of the extension depends on the size of the button. Generally, you'll want to add half the width of the button plus ¼" (6mm).

Trace the front sloper piece. Add half the size of the button, plus ¼" (6mm), to the center front. Add the seam allowance.

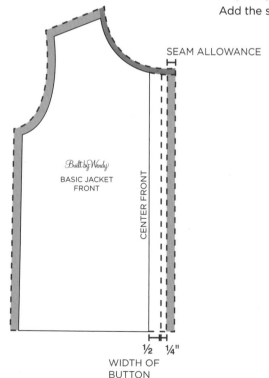

SEAM ALLOWANCE

Built by Wendy
BASIC JACKET
FRONT

CENTER FRONT

½ ¼"
WIDTH OF
BUTTON

YOUR HOLEYNESS: *HOW TO MARK BUTTONHOLES*

Most buttonholes on coats and jackets are placed horizontally so that there's some wiggle room in the fit of the coat. If they are placed vertically, they can pull a bit and ruin the clean look of the jacket.

On each front piece, mark a cross where your button will be placed. The buttons will be sewn on one side and the buttonholes sewn on the other side.

On the side where the buttonholes will be sewn, measure out the size of your button plus ⅛" (3mm). Make another cross mark.

Mark a horizontal line between the crosses—that's your buttonhole!

TIP:

Use pins, an awl, or your marking pen to note where the buttonholes go on the pattern.

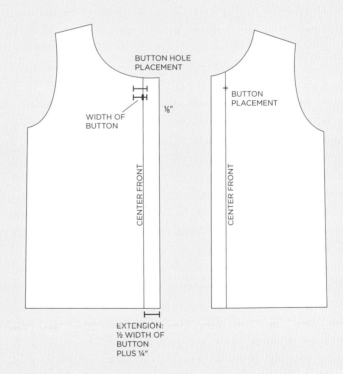

BUTTON HOLE
PLACEMENT

WIDTH OF
BUTTON

⅛"

BUTTON
PLACEMENT

CENTER FRONT

CENTER FRONT

EXTENSION:
½ WIDTH OF
BUTTON
PLUS ¼"

bits and pieces CONTINUED

Zipper Extension

Even though a zipper can be inserted down the center front of the jacket, sometimes you may want to cover the zipper with an extension—either for style or for function (because no one likes cold wind seeping through their zipper teeth). The extension can also go inside behind the zipper to protect your skin from being pinched. Confused? Check out your favorite parka to see what I'm talking about. The width of the extension can be whatever you want, but they are generally 1" to 3" (2.5cm to 7.5cm) wide.

1. Extend the center front by the desired measurement, for example, by 2" (5cm) for a 2" (5cm) wide extension.

2. Cut the extension and the front pieces apart at the center line.

3. Label the outer edge of the extension "on fold."

4. Add the seam allowance to the new edge, including its top and bottom.

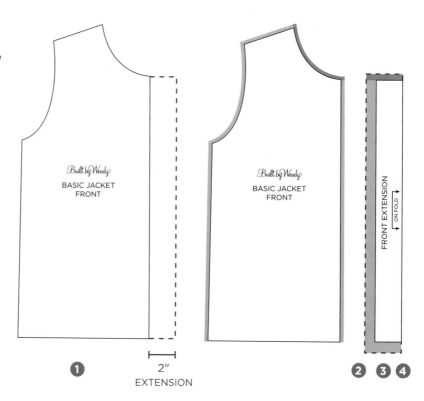

Built by Wendy
BASIC JACKET
FRONT

❶

2"
EXTENSION

Built by Wendy
BASIC JACKET
FRONT

FRONT EXTENSION
ON FOLD

❷ ❸ ❹

> **TIP:**
> Try the combination of a zipper extension with some snaps attached to hold it closed. You see this look a lot in activewear—it's super functional, and looks sporty chic, too.

COLLARS AND HOODS

Playing with the shape of these pieces is a fun way to make them more dramatic and really alter the design of a coat or jacket. Try changing the shape of the collar point or the curve of the hood, or vary the height of the piece by adding a few inches (5cm–10cm) to make an oversized, face-framing collar or a drapey, Stevie Nicks–style hood.

CUFFS

A classic shirt cuff—the kind that has a button closure with a placket—is used on shirts but also appears on classic jean jackets and army jackets. To make one, first choose the width of the cuff. Most sportswear jacket cuffs range from 1″ to 3″ (2.5cm to 7.5cm). The slimmer you make it, the more delicate the jacket will look.

1. Trace the sleeve sloper.

2. Make a horizontal line 2″ (5cm) above the sleeve opening.

3. Cut off this piece.

4. Remove 1″ (2.5cm) from the length of this piece.

5. Add the seam allowances.

6. On the sleeve, mark a 4″ (10cm) vertical line located 2″ (5cm) in from the back side seam.

7. Then make a mark 1″ (2.5cm) away from the line. Add another mark 1″ (2.5cm) away. These will be the pleat marks.

8. Add the seam allowances.

9. For the sleeve placket, make an 8″ × 1½″ (24cm × 3.8cm) piece.

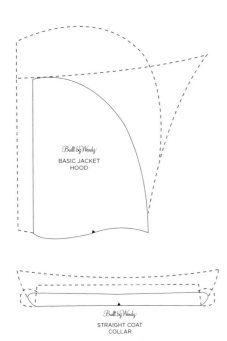

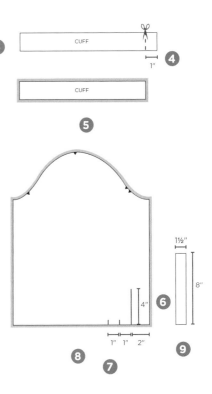

TO HAVE AND TO HOLD: POCKETS

Pockets are not only functional, they're also a great way to personalize your design. Before creating your own, of course, you must decide where you want them. You can insert an inseam pocket wherever there is a seam. Usually these pockets are put at hip level in the side seam of a coat. Many jackets have patch pockets, which can be made in any shape you want. They can also have flaps, which can also be made in any shape. Triangle? Half moon? Why not? And they can have a closure, or not. Pockets can be so fun to play with since there are very few constraints—they're one of my favorite tricks to make an old style feel new again. Don't be afraid to think outside the rectangle!

TIP:

To draw the inseam pocket, I simply place my hand on the pattern area where the pocket should be, and trace a rounded shape around my hand!

Top Open Patch

This is the most classic type of pocket, and so easy to make—just draw a basic square or rectangle, rounding the edges if desired. Add a hem at the top—generally 1″ (2.5cm) wide—and ½″ (13mm) seam allowances around the sides.

Pocket flaps can be any shape or size, but they're usually the same width as the pocket they are covering. Feel free to play with pointed or curved corners, make them any height you want, and place interesting closures on them (like fun vintage buttons or tough work wear-style hardware). Instead of placing one button in the middle, try two—one on each corner. Feel free to play around!

Side Open Patch

This is a fun sportswear-inspired look that is functional, too. Just draw the shape, add ½″ (13mm) seam allowances, and mark with notches where your hand will slip in. Make sure it's wide enough for your hand, plus a bit on either side.

Inseam pockets are great because they are hidden (which makes for a sleeker, dressier vibe). Trace onto the sloper piece where you want the pocket to go, mark on your seam where your hand will naturally slip in, and then draw the shape of a pocket (rounded corners are better, to prevent pileup of random bits of

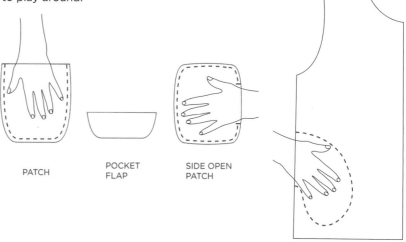

PATCH

POCKET FLAP

SIDE OPEN PATCH

INSEAM

junk). Add the seam allowances, and you're ready to go. You can always change one of the jacket projects this way, using inseam pockets as opposed to adding visible patch pockets.

Kangaroo Pocket

The easiest way to make one of these is to look at your existing hoodies to see the size and shape, take measurements, and hand-draw a new pattern piece. You can switch up the shape however you like, but make sure the pocket openings are big enough to put your hands in.

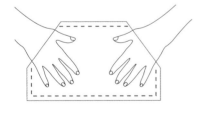

KANGAROO

RUFFLES

Ruffles are easy to make and hard to ignore—they add a fun, feminine twist to a coat's hem, sleeve hem, front openings, or collar (in fact, they can be inserted basically anywhere there's a seam). For such a dramatic design changer, the pattern is incredibly simple: Just make a long, thin rectangle according to your desired size.

1. Figure out the width of your ruffle. Say you want it to be 2" (5cm) wide. Double that, since this piece will be folded in half, and make it 4" (10cm) wide.

2. Measure the length of the area where you want to insert the ruffle. Say it's 10" (25.5cm). Since you will be gathering this piece to form the ruffle, you'll generally double that measurement as well, unless you want an extremely dense or barely ruffled ruffle. Generally speaking, for this opening, your ruffle would be 20" (51cm) long.

3. Add the seam allowances.

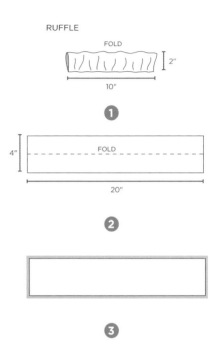

BELTS AND CARRIERS

I love cozy, oversized jackets and coats, but I hate feeling like an Oompa Loompa. Belts enable you to create an hourglass silhouette even when you're bundled up. They make trench coats and wrap coats chic and flattering, and they're also a fun way to play with contrast colors and textures (try a leatherette belt with corduroy or velvet belt on a classic wool coat). You can even attach them in unusual places—why not put a belt along the bottom of a swingy coat to add the option of a balloon silhouette? As a design alternative to the standard thin strip, you may even want to make the piece thick, like a sash, to form a big bow (picture a voluminous silk charmeuse cincher on a bouclé dinner jacket). You can also attach a buckle or some sort of closure to the end of the belt as desired.

Since belts are usually pretty long, and most fabrics are not as wide as the belt length, you will need to make a shorter pattern piece, one that is one-quarter the length of your belt; place it on the fold of the fabric twice, and sew the pieces together so that the belt has a center back seam. Widthwise, you can make a belt any width you want, but I usually like my belts between 1" and 3" (2.5cm–7.5cm) wide so that it's easy to tie the ends in a knot or sew them through any of the variety of premade belt buckles that are available in the stores. The width of the belt needs to be doubled since you are folding it in half, so if you want a belt 2" (5cm) wide you would make the piece 4"(10cm) wide.

BELT

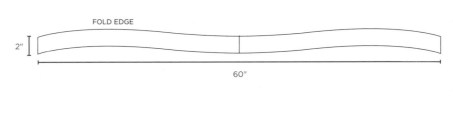

a snip in time

A GUIDE TO CUTTING WITHOUT CUTTING CORNERS

Carriers—pieces that function as belt loops—can be any size you want, from a tiny vertical rectangle to an oversized tunnel. Just make sure the belt fits inside!

Belt: 2" wide × 60" long (5cm × 152.5cm)
1. Make the pattern piece 4" (10cm) wide × 15" (38cm) long.

2. Add the seam allowances and label "on the fold" on one short end of the piece.

Carrier: ½" wide × 2½" long (13mm × 6.5cm)
1. Make the pattern piece 1" (2.5cm) wide × 2½" (6.5cm) long.

2. Add ¼" (6mm) seam allowances to the width and ½" (13mm) seam allowances to the length.

CARRIER

2½"

2½"

Can't wait to bust out the scissors and take your pattern pieces from paper to 3-D? Not so fast! The last step before sewing is just as important as the sewing itself. Everything from preparing the fabric to placing the pattern pieces must be done slowly and carefully, or you may find that your new corduroy peacoat has lines pointing in all directions. I've said it in every one of my other books, and I'll say it again: Think twice, cut once! In the following pages, we'll go over the steps necessary to prepare fabric and pattern pieces, figure out how to handle special fabrics, place pattern pieces on fabric, securing and cutting, and storing the cut pieces so that they'll stay together even when you don't have time to finish your project. Now, chop-chop!

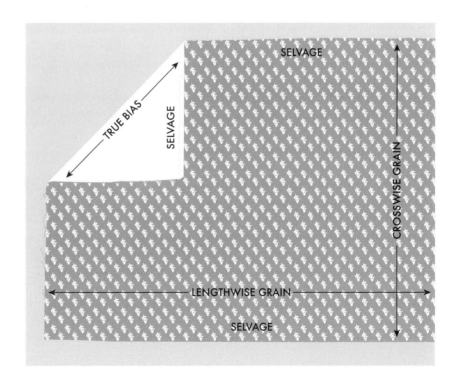

doubling up
FOLDING FABRIC

Fold the fabric in half, selvage to selvage and face to face. The face of the fabric should be folded on the inside, so that any markings you make will be on the wrong side of the garment.

SECURITY CHECKPOINT:

SPECIAL FABRIC CONSIDERATIONS FOR CUTTING

Fabric Face

Most fabrics have a right side and wrong side. The right side is the "face" of the fabric, and the wrong side is the "back." You must always determine which side is the face, and make sure you cut accordingly; nothing is more infuriating, or more easily preventable, than a fuzzy alpaca coat with a back that isn't fuzzy! With prints and napped fabrics, the face is easy to find, but in some fabrics it's more difficult to discern. Hold the fabric up to bright light, inspect it carefully, and decide which side looks more appealing. Many fabrics have labeling on the selvage, so that will make the case clear. In some cases, it won't matter too much (as long as you cut consistently on one side or the other!) while in others, you may want to break the rules; a deliberately inside-out faux fur, for instance, could look avant-garde cool (and feel nice and fluffy inside, to boot).

Direction

Some fabrics have a specific direction. With prints you can usually tell if it's a "one-way" design (arrows, stripes, words, or even houndstooth), which has to be cut differently than an allover design, in which the pattern looks the same viewed from different angles, such as polka dots. If you're going to work with a one-way print, be sure to buy extra fabric, because you have to lay all of the pattern pieces in the same direction. Otherwise you'll end up with a jacket with the front upside down and the back right side up!

Other fabrics, like corduroy, velvet, and shaggy qualities, have a nap, meaning that the yarns fall smoother in one direction and coarser in the other. Light hits napped fabric in different ways depending on the direction of the yarns, so it's important to cut all the patterns pieces in the same direction. Otherwise, some components of your coat will appear darker and others lighter, or the mohair of one sleeve may go up instead of down!

Matching Plaids, Stripes, and Patterns

When placing pattern pieces on any of these types of fabrics, line up the notches and the bottom edges of the pattern pieces along any horizontal lines of the print. This way, the print will look correct on every piece of the garment, instead of askew and amateurish.

puzzle pieces
PLACING THE PATTERN ONTO FABRIC

When you place the pattern pieces onto the fabric for cutting, try to squeeze the pieces as close together as possible, but make sure you can fit them all in. I've created recommended layouts for the coat and jacket ideas in this book, and these will be helpful for determining layouts for your own project ideas. However, keep in mind that if your fabric is unusually narrow or has a one-way design or nap, you may have to move some things around (and buy extra fabric!), and if your fabric is one-way in direction, you'll have to place all the pieces in the same direction.

GETTING ATTACHED

Securing Pattern Pieces to Fabric
If you don't take steps to keep pattern pieces in place as you cut, they'll scoot around, ruining the shape of your pattern pieces! My favorite method is to place weights all over the pattern pieces—something as simple as a soup can or paperweight works just fine in a pinch. You can also use pins to secure the corners, but this is time-consuming and sometimes difficult

if you are cutting heavy wool fabric. Once you're accustomed to cutting, you'll probably find (as I have) that a combination of weights and your fingers is the fastest and easiest method, and still precise. When using pins, always insert each pin into the seam allowance area of the pattern—rather than inside the seam line and onto the body of the garment—so as not to ruin the fabric, especially if you'll be working with a delicate open weave (such as a lightweight summer linen).

DOUBLE TROUBLE: *A WORD ABOUT CUTTING ON THE FOLD*

Since cutting is done with patterns laid onto folded fabric, you are cutting two layers at once. That makes it a great time saver—but for pattern pieces like a back of the coat which only have one symmetrical piece instead of two, you'll need to lay the piece on the fold of the fabric. When you cut the half-pattern piece and open it up, the fabric will form one symmetrical piece. When you see patterns that should be cut this way, they are noted with "on the fold". Don't let this instruction get past you, or you'll end up with two halves instead of one whole!

TIP:

Double-check that all pattern pieces specified in the book to be cut "on the fold" are placed carefully along the fold of the fabric. This is generally the case for back pieces, since the fronts of almost all jackets and coats are open. If you're creating your own design, consult a similar style in the project chapters if you aren't sure what to do.

snip to it!

CUTTING

Just before you cut, make a checklist using the previous points in this section. Did you place things correctly for this type of fabric? Are the pieces meant to be on the fold actually on the fold? Remember, think twice, cut once! Using sharp shears, cut the fabric pieces out slowly and carefully along the pattern edges, making sure that the pattern pieces don't move around.

1. Get your supplies ready: Fabric scissors, weights, pins, and washable marker or chalk.

2. Fold the fabric in half, selvage to selvage and face to face.

3. Check any special properties of your fabric. Is it one-way or does it have a print? If so, keep this in mind as you....

4. Place pattern pieces on the fabric.

5. Double-check that pattern pieces specified "on the fold" are placed on the fold, and that all piec es follow the grainline.

6. Secure pattern pieces to the fabric with weights or pins. If using pins, keep them within the seam allowance only.

7. Double-check one more time that everything is laid out correctly for the type of fabric and the type of pattern piece.

8. And...cut!

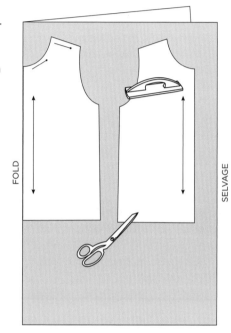

FOLD

SELVAGE

TIP:

Make sure that all patterns are placed on the grain, or the finished product may look off (and, depending on the fabric, behave strangely). The grainline marking on the patterns should run parallel to the selvage edge of the fabric.

TIP:

If a heavy coat fabric is too thick to cut through two layers at once, you can instead carefully slip your scissors under one layer and cut it first. Then cut the next layer underneath it.

make your mark

ADDING NOTCHES AND MARKINGS

Now that the pieces have been cut, add markings immediately—before you forget what's what! Using the tip of your scissors, gently clip any and all notches into their designated seam allowance areas as reflected on the pattern pieces, being careful not to cut past the seam line into the body of the garment. For pocket placement markings, use a washable pen, chalk, or pin—whatever you've already tested to prove that it won't damage the fabric—to designate the spot.

bundles of joy

KEEPING CUT PIECES ORGANIZED

Jackets and coats are time-consuming projects, and more often than not the process gets spread out over days (or weeks, or even months!). If you're not planning to sew your jacket or coat right away, make sure your efforts don't go to waste, and keep all your carefully cut pieces together and stowed away. My favorite method (and the one used by factories, too): Leaving the pattern pieces on top of their corresponding cut pieces, place each piece of the garment into one neat stack, and roll the entire bundle up like you're making cinnamon rolls. Tie it together with a ribbon or rubber band, and label it very clearly. Otherwise, you never know—your nearsighted roommate might mistake it for a bundle of rags and use it to scrub the bathroom!

TIP:

For busy girls like me, storage is key. I like to throw the bundle in a large plastic Ziploc bag to protect the fabric, and then draw a quick sketch of the style and slip that into the bag with any trims. Then, when I'm ready to sew, it's all there for me, with no chance of confusion. It may sound excessive, but trust me, nothing is a bigger bummer than losing a sleeve or two, or spilling coffee onto what you thought was a scrap pile and discovering you've ruined your precious white cashmere pattern pieces!

CHAPTER 3

IN STITCHES

SEWING NOTES FOR COATS AND JACKETS

SEWING IS A LOT LIKE YOGA. ONCE YOU'VE LEARNED THE STEPS, going through the motions is meditative bliss—but lose focus, and you might blow a knee (or a needle). If we continue with this analogy, I guess you might say that sewing coats and jackets is the equivalent of crow pose or a headstand: seemingly a bit complicated, but with patience and dedication, totally attainable. And I'm your instructor, here to guide you!

In this chapter I'll show you the important sewing pointers—my favorite secrets and shortcuts gleaned from years of having my own line and making stuff on the side—that we'll use for the book projects, ideas specifically helpful for sewing the types of seams, trims, and other components commonly found on coats and jackets.

I've written this chapter more as a supplementary lesson geared to sewing outerwear than an exhaustively detailed guide for greenhorns. If the only Singer you're familiar with is Beyoncé, then I strongly encourage you to get your feet wet making a few practice muslins with your machine before you break out the wool-cashmere felt.

Sewing a coat, as we've gone over, is like building a house, and it's easiest to think of it as a three-step process. First you have to do the construction so that it's held together and stable—in this case, that means creating seams (attaching parts together). Then it's time for the painting, moldings, and floors to cover up the rough stuff—in this case that means finishing the openings at the sleeve (cuffs), neck (collars and hoods), bottom (hems), front (facings), and inside (linings). After that comes the decoration—not essential for its existence, but the things that make it functional and make it you: hanging pictures and lighting, putting down rugs. For clothes, it means creating closures like zippers or buttonholes, and adding trims like elastic and piping. This chapter is packed with useful tidbits for each stage, so let's get going!

gear up
SUPPLIES

Don't just grab 'em and go: Especially when shopping for outerwear supplies, it's crucial to get the right sizes and qualities for the type of fabric you're using (denim will need a denim-weight needle, and so on). Also, don't even think about getting started until your machine is oiled up and your iron is clean. A few minutes now will save a few headaches later!

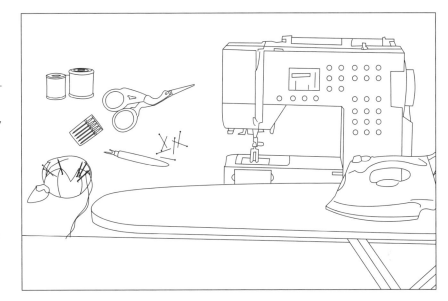

Machine needles: Make sure you get the right size for your fabric. Super-light fabrics use size 9 (65) or 11 (75). A medium-weight fabric for a lighter jacket (like a cotton canvas or poplin) will take size 11 (75) or 14 (90); medium-heavy fabric (denim, felt, or leather) will require size 14 (90) or 16 (100); upholstery or heavy-duty cotton duck works best with size 18 (110).

Hand needles: The hand-stitching you'll do—buttons and such—requires fabric-appropriate needles, too. The size numbers go down instead of up: Airy fabrics use size 9 or 10; lightweight silks and cottons use 8 or 9; medium-weight fabrics take a 7 or 8; medium-heavy fabrics need a 6 or 7; and for seriously heavy and dense fabrics, you'll take anything from a 1 to 5.

Thread: All-purpose thread works for sewing most fabrics, except for the very light (use extra-fine thread) or very heavy (use topstitching-grade thread for seams). For topstitching, use topstitching thread

Scissors: Basic fabric shears are a must for clipping threads and any small trimming, and fabric.

Straight pins: These are essential for pinning pieces together while sewing. I like the kind with colored balls on the tips—they're easier to see and to work with.

Seam ripper: This nifty little tool is for opening up basting or ripping out any mistakes. I find that they tend to disappear easily, so I suggest picking up more than one!

Sewing machine: Read your machine's instructions. Make sure the machine is well oiled and all the settings are correct for your project. Don't try to cut corners on getting the machine ready—you'll end up wasting more time than you saved in the first place.

Iron and board: Set up your board and keep your iron filled with water and heated up so that you can easily press your seams. No one likes to have to break their concentration to get a new step set up in the middle of sewing.

18" (45.5cm) clear ruler: It's always good to have one on hand to check the measurements, especially when folding back hems and placing pockets.

come together

A PRIMER ON SEWING SEAMS

STEP 1: SECURING

Place the pieces to be joined with their right sides together. That term, which will pop up often in the project chapters, means that the face of the fabric is "kissing" the face of the other piece. (This setup is also sometimes called "face to face.") Insert the pins into the area that is part of the seam allowance. (Remember that ½" [13mm] you added to your pattern pieces?) The pins should be perpendicular to the seam so that they're easy to pull out as you sew.

STEP 2: PLACING

Making sure that your machine and bobbin are properly threaded, pull out a few inches (5cm-10cm) of the top thread and the bobbin thread, and place them behind the raised presser foot. Place the fabric pieces under the presser foot along the seam allowance guide marked ½" (13mm).

STEP 3: SEWING

Lower the presser foot and sew a few stitches, then reverse over them for a few stitches to secure your start of the seam. Keep sewing until you get to the end of the piece. Once you get to the end, reverse again for a few stitches to secure the end of the seam. Clip the loose threads with scissors.

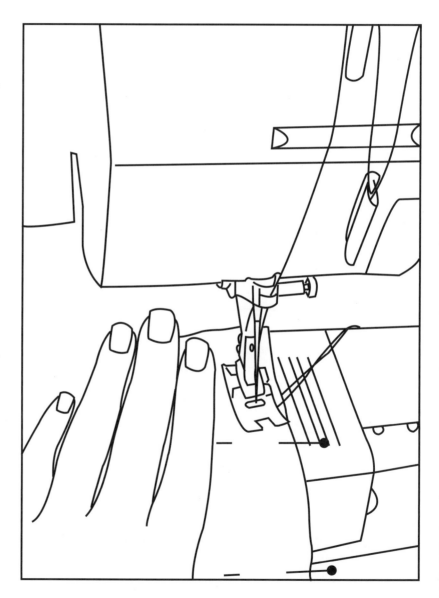

THE UNUSUAL SUSPECTS: *SPECIAL SEAMS*

Curved

Curved seams make jackets and coats conform to your body's contours, but handling them isn't a straight-and-narrow proposition. In any curved seam, one piece of fabric will curve inward and one will curve outward. Because of this, the seam allowances will behave strangely once the seam is sewn. On the inward curve, the allowance will bunch up, and on the outward curve, it will be stretched taut. How to handle the situation? Your scissors can help. Once you have stitched each piece, clip (for inward curves) or notch (for outward curves) just inside the seam allowance at regular intervals from the raw edge, getting close to the stitch line—but do not cut the stitch line! This will create space for overlapping fabric on the inward curve, and open up space on the outward curve. This technique will be used primarily for sewing princess seams and set-in sleeve caps.

Gathered

When making jackets and coats, there might be times when you'll have to gather up a larger amount of fabric and stitch

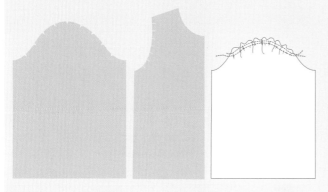

it into a smaller space; this is the basic principle of a gathered seam. You'll use this technique for puffed cap sleeves and some places on the body of garments made of lightweight fabric. It's very difficult to gather heavy wool and other thick fabrics, so my advice is not to bother trying ruched, shirred, or pleated styles with felt or fur.

1. Set your machine stitch length to the longest option.

2. Sew a row of stitching ¼" (6mm) away from the raw edge, then another ⅝" (16mm) away from the first row.

3. Pull the bottom threads (those that came from the bobbin) and, using your fingers, slowly push the fabric along the threads so that it gathers.

4. Pin this gathered piece to the appropriate piece of flat fabric (this will be the bottom or sleeve opening if you're making a ruffled hem or cuff, for instance) with the right sides together. Maneuver the gathers so that they fit into the space evenly.

5. Using a regular length stitch, sew a seam in between the gathering rows you stitched before, positioning this new seam closer to the second row—about ½" (13mm) from the raw edge.

6. Remove the second row of thread, which will be showing through on the garment. The first row of thread is now encased inside the seam allowance.

Basting

This is a technique using very long stitches—the longest on your machine. Basting is used to make a temporary seam, which will be ripped out later. What's the point, then? It's instrumental for sewing zippers and gathering ruffles, both of which we'll cover later.

coming clean

FINISHING SEAM ALLOWANCES

After you sew each seam, you must finish the raw edge of the seam allowance and press the seam. This prevents it from unraveling and just looks and feels a whole lot nicer! This step is unnecessary, however, if you plan on fully lining your coat or jacket, because the lining will hide the raw seams.

SERGING

A serger cuts a fabric edge and wraps it with thread at the same time. If you have the machine, it's a quick, though not particularly attractive, way to keep raw edges in check. If you don't have one, keep reading.

PINKING

Simply trimming the raw edges with pinking shears—scissors that create a zigzag edge—is enough to keep many fabrics in line. The zigzag line can even have a decorative feeling for non-fray-prone fabrics like faux suede (you may even want to sew the seams inside out!).

ZIGZAG

Running a zigzag stitch from your regular machine along the seam allowance works in a pinch to keep seam allowances from unraveling. It's not ideal for coats you'll be living in, though; for those, binding is a sturdier and better-looking long-term option.

BINDING

This technique basically means encasing the raw edge inside thin strips of bias-cut fabric, whether store-bought or homemade. It can be folded, wrapped around the raw edge, and stitched down, sealing the unsightly seam allowance inside. Binding is a super professional-looking option for unlined jackets, and it's a great place to play with design, too, since it highlights the seaming of the garment. A contrast color or print—like a bright Schiaparelli pink inside a classic peacoat, or a cute madras plaid inside a khaki version—can be the extra detail that takes your jacket from standard to spectacular.

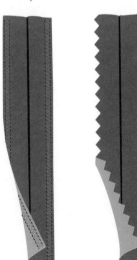

hemming and hawing
FINISHING RAW OPENINGS

The final step in sewing is to cover up any of the raw edges of the garment's openings:

- Bottom
- Front
- Sleeve
- Armhole (if the jacket is sleeveless)
- Neck

You can choose from the following ways to finish each opening (or, technically, hem them—they're all hems, not just the bottom). We'll go over each in detail, but first here's a list of your options.

- Hem
- Facing
- Binding
- Trim
- Lining
- Additional construction pieces

BOTTOMS UP: TYPES OF HEMS

The thickness of a garment's hem depends on several factors: the shape of the hem, the fabric type, and how you want it to look. No matter what type of hem you're sewing, one thing is crucial: You must measure and press it carefully, or else the garment will look messy. Keep your clear ruler at hand, and make use of it. Check and recheck to make sure the line isn't sloping at an angle, and try the garment on before you sew.

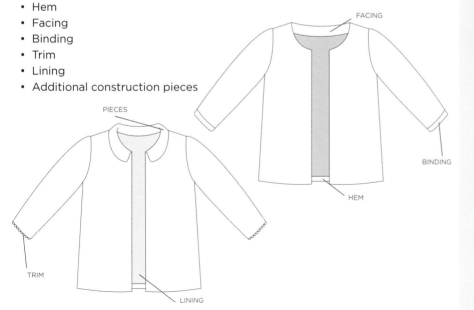

PIECES

TRIM

LINING

FACING

BINDING

HEM

HEM FINISHES

You can finish the raw edge of your hem with either a basic finish or clean finish. A basic finish is fast and easy: You can use pinking shears, a serger overlock stitch, or a conventional machine zigzag stitch to finish the raw edge before turning it back for the hem. This saves time if you're whipping something up to wear tonight, but it doesn't look so nice. For a more professional look, you can use a clean finish, for which you fold back the raw edge once—usually about a ¼" (6mm)—and then you fold up the hem and sew it.

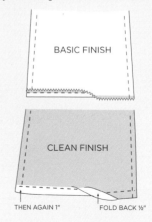

BASIC FINISH

CLEAN FINISH

THEN AGAIN 1"   FOLD BACK ½"

Blindstitch hem

As the name suggests, this hem doesn't look like a hem at all. That's because only one out of every few stitches pokes through to the outer surface, so that no stitching lines are visible on the garment. It makes for a cleaner, more professional look, especially if you're working with fine fabrics and going for a high-end vibe (say, a cashmere-angora wrap coat to wear to an important meeting). It also requires a special blindstitch hem presser foot for your sewing machine, so be sure to have one ready before you sit down to sew!

1. Fold back the seam allowance, which will generally be ½" (13mm).

2. Fold back the width of the hem.

3. Fold back the garment so that the edge of the hem peeks out.

4. With the wrong side of the garment up, slip the lip under your blindstitch hem foot, and stitch the hem, keeping the straight stitches on the hem and letting the zigzag bites grab the main garment fabric.

TIP:

What's invisible on the outside can be fun to make visible on the inside. Try covering a blindstitched hem's seam allowance with contrast binding or a pretty ribbon for a surprise detail that will peek out from time to time.

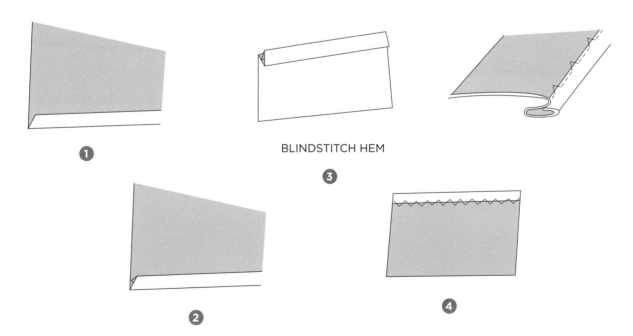

BLINDSTITCH HEM

❶

❷

❸

❹

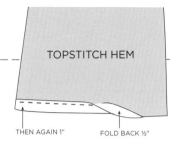

TOPSTITCH HEM

THEN AGAIN 1"   FOLD BACK ½"

Topstitch hem

This hem, as the name suggests, has a visible stitch line on the outside of the garment. This is the classic hem used in sportswear and can also be sewn with contrast thread for a fun detail. It's not exactly dressy, but it's sturdy, and will work just fine for most projects that utilize casual fabrics, such as army and jean jackets. For a 1" (2.5cm) hem do as follows:

1. Fold back the seam allowance ½" (13mm).

2. Fold back the width of the hem 1" (2.5cm).

3. Pin the hem, turn the garment over, press, and stitch on the face of the garment at a measurement ⅛" (3mm) less than the hem width, or ⅞" (2.2cm) for this hem.

TIP:

It's not great to topstitch onto napped fabrics like corduroy, velvet, and fluffy wools because the stitch line will sink into the fabric and create a heavy, noticeable line. Try a blindstitch hem instead.

END GAME: *ABOUT HEMS FOR OPENINGS*

Bottom and Sleeves

These are the typical places for hems to be sewn. In fact, we mainly refer to the bottom opening as the "hem." Depending on the look and fabric weight—bigger fabric usually demands bigger hems, and vice versa—you can make a hem anywhere from ½" (13mm) to 4" (10cm). The wider the hem, the harder it can be to handle and sew straight. Make sure to use plenty of pins to hold a wide hem in place as you sew. Sometimes it's good to add a piece of interfacing in the hem to keep things stable.

Center Front

If you're not using any closures on the front of your jacket, then it's okay to simply hem the front opening. It's nicer to use a facing, though. If you do plan on having closures, you'll have to make the opening sturdy enough to carry them. If you want to go the hem route, make it wide and add interfacing inside to stabilize it, so that wooden toggles or big brass buttons don't drag you down.

Armholes and Neck

Hemming this area is a tricky proposition because these areas are usually curved, and therefore pretty difficult to fold back on themselves. If the armhole is made to be a straight opening (as with the raglan sleeve pattern), then a hem is fine, but otherwise, a facing or binding might make more sense. Depending on the fabric and style, you can make any size hem you want in these areas (although a huge hem on a curved opening is a recipe for frustration).

doubling up
SEWING FACINGS

Generally, a facing is made of the same fabric as the garment. (It's always a good idea to apply interfacing—a stabilizing iron-on webbed fabric—to the wrong side of the facing to keep it from flipping around, wrinkling, and bunching). Here's how to sew it on:

1. Attach the interfacing to the wrong side of the facing.

2. With right sides together, sew the front facing to the back facing at the shoulders.

3. Finish the raw edge of the facing with a serger, pinking shears, or zigzag stitch (that's the edge that is not being joined to the body of the garment).

4. With right sides together, sew the facing to the body around the front and the neckline.

5. Press the seam allowance toward the facing, and understitch it down.

6. To prevent the facing from flipping out, you'll also need to secure it inside the garment. You can do this by hand-stitching the facing to the shoulder seam or side seam. Or you can use your machine's blindstitch function to secure the entire facing to the body. (This is a bit time consuming, but it looks nice and clean and will keep unwanted flaps of facing from showing their faces.)

FACINGS FOR OPENINGS

Bottom and Sleeves

You'll mainly use a facing for the bottom or sleeve opening if the opening is curved, which makes a hem difficult to fold (unless the hem width is small, less than ½″ [13mm]). If you have a very wide hem, it's also good to make the bottom hem as a facing to save on the fabric yardage. Also, you might want to utilize facings here for a design effect. Why not use electric purple facing to finish the bottom and sleeves of a black coat?

> **TIP:**
>
> To finish facing, you can cover the raw edge with some binding, or just fold back the seam allowance and topstitch. Sometimes the facing is attached to a lining piece, so that will actually finish the edge for you.

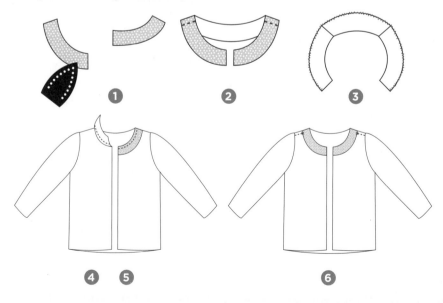

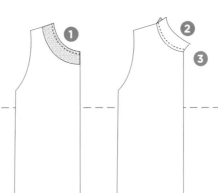

Front

Most fronts are finished with a facing, which is stabilized with interfacing. This makes the front stiff enough to support buttons or other closures. This piece is usually combined with the front neck facing.

Armholes and Neck

These areas are normally faced, too—especially the neckline in designer outerwear. When the coat or jacket is hanging on a hanger, the first thing you see inside is the back of the neck, and it looks nicer if you see the fabric and not the lining. Facing the neck and armholes (for sleeveless styles only) also adds support, so that the garment doesn't look or feel flimsy. It will hold its shape better on a hanger, and possibly on you.

USING UNDERSTITCHING TO SECURE FACINGS

This technique is generally used in neck and armhole facings, and involves edgestitching the seam allowance to another part of the garment (in this case, that's the facing). Understitching is used to secure the facing (or other piece) in place so that it stays in line with the body of the garment and doesn't flip over.

1. With right sides together, stitch the facing to the garment opening.

2. Press the seam allowance towards the facing.

3. Topstitch the facing onto the face, ¼" (6mm) from the seam (this is

also known as "edgestitching"—see the topstitching sidebar on page 77), capturing the garment's seam allowance layers underneath.

INTERFACING FOR OUTERWEAR

When finishing openings with facings, it's pretty much a given that the pieces should have interfacing attached to the wrong side. This keeps the garment stable and, as we've gone over, supports the weight and stress of closures that might be placed onto that part of the body.

If a hem is very wide, generally wider than 3" (7.5cm), it's also a good idea to use interfacing to keep the area tidy and stable.

Also, in the case of many coats and jackets, the entire front body pieces of the garment will have interfacing. This gives the jacket a nice, structured finish, and helps it hold up heavy pockets and flaps.

Sometimes, as I mentioned earlier, I'll use interfacing throughout my entire coat if the fabric doesn't seem as heavy and stiff as I would like it. Flimsy coats look cheap, so it's never a bad idea to use interfacing on all your pieces. It may take a bit more time now, but it will make the finished product look like a million bucks.

inside edition

SEWING LININGS

A lining not only makes a coat look and feel more high quality, but it is actually quite functional. The smooth face of the lining makes it quicker to slip into (it's always a bummer when your sweater sleeves get bunched up inside your coat) and prevents pesky static in the winter. It also makes the jacket or coat a bit warmer. For lighter or more casual coats and jackets, it's not necessary, but if you are making a nice wool coat or anything with an itchy fabric, it's best to line it. See page 43 for a refresher on making patterns for the lining pieces.

1. With right sides together, sew the front lining to the back lining at the shoulders.

2. With right sides together, sew the sleeve linings to the lining armholes.

3. With right sides together, sew the lining front to the lining back at the side seams from the bottom opening up to the sleeve opening.

4. Hem the bottom opening of the lining.

5. Attach the interfacing to the facings. With right sides together, sew the front facing to the back facing at the shoulders.

6. With right sides together, sew the lining to the facing around the neckline and fronts.

7. With right sides together, sew the garment to the facing around the neckline and fronts. Sew the front facing to the bottom along the width of the hem.

8. Turn the garment right side out, then fold up the hem of the the bottom opening and hand-stitch the lining's bottom opening to the garment hem.

9. Fold back the sleeve opening and sleeve lining, opening the hems, and hand-stitch them together.

LININGS FOR OPENINGS

Bottom and Sleeves

A lining in this area is most likely attached to the hems of these areas. If you look inside one of your coats or jackets, you will notice that the garment fabric is folded back at least 1" (2.5cm) inside of the coat, and then the lining is attached to that. If you have a beautiful printed silk lining that you're trying to show off, however, you could also attach the lining directly to the garment without a hem.

Front, Armholes, and Neck

Most jacket and coat fronts are not lined all the way to the edge without a facing attached. You can do it, but in that case I would recommend putting interfacing behind the lining to keep things sturdier.

FINGER LOOKIN' GOOD: *HOW TO HAND-STITCH SUCCESSFULLY*

Call it laziness or just a lack of eye-hand coordination, but I'm just not a big fan of hand-stitching, and anytime I can avoid it, I will. Still, with outerwear especially, there are times when it's necessary, such as when you're attaching a lining to the sleeve or bottom opening of your garment, or attaching a facing or lining to a zippered front closure. Here's how to do it right:

1. Fold back the seam allowance of the lining or facing piece and pin it to the seam allowance of the sleeve or bottom opening hem, or zipper tape.

2. Thread the needle (see the buttons section, page 80, in this chapter for detailed instructions if you need help).

3. Slide the needle diagonally up through the garment hem and then through the lining's seam allowance. Continue stitching, leaving ¼" (6mm) of space between each stitch. Use a thimble to protect your thumb, if you're feeling sensitive.

strip tips

MAKING AND ATTACHING BIAS BINDING

USING BINDINGS TO FINISH OPENINGS

Bottom, Sleeves, Front, Armholes, and Neck

Binding works great as an alternative to hemming and facing on all these areas. You can make a soft, drapey jacket with no lining and facings and just use binding, which will keep it less stiff. If you make a stiffer coat that has lining and facing, like a peacoat, it is still easy to cover the seams where the lining and facing meet with binding. A contrasting binding can really liven up a basic coat, accentuating its construction (and showing off your skills in the process). These days, there are so many choices in metallics, faux leather, and unique textures—why stick to basic black?

Bias binding (also known as bias tape) is a strip of fabric that wraps around a raw edge to finish it. You can buy basic solid colors at the store, but it's more fun to make your own if you feel like getting creative. Store-bought binding already comes with its edges folded inside cleanly, so simply slip your garment's raw edge inside the folds of the binding and edgestitch it. Start and finish at a seam—that way, the binding seam will be less conspicuous.

Homemade binding is made using a bias tape maker (one of my all-time favorite inventions) or by carefully folding a 1"- (2.5cm-) wide strip of fabric cut along the bias. Feed the strip through the bias tape maker, or to make tape manually, prepare it by pressing the strip in half, and then fold under both raw edges to the center along the length of the binding. Then, insert the raw edge of the garment into the folded piece, and edgestitch the binding down.

TIP:

Bias binding is great for finishing seams on boiled wool or double-faced cashmere coats, when you don't want to face or line the fabric—you want to show it off!

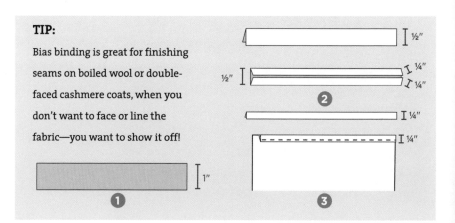

piece signs

ATTACHING COLLARS, HOODS, CUFFS, AND OTHER PIECES

Most neck and sleeve openings are finished with additional pieces, such as a collar, hood, or cuff. Here's how to handle them.

COLLARS

This is the most classic way to finish a coat at the neck. Since most coats and jackets are used as a layer for warmth, it's nice to have a collar to cover your neck, of course. Collars also frame your face and accentuate your features!

1. Attach interfacing (iron-on fusible interfacing is best) to the wrong side of the collar piece.

2. With right sides together, sew the collar pieces together around the outer edge.

3. Trim the seam allowance at the corners, and turn the collar around. Press the collar flat and topstitch around the outer edge.

TIP:

When sewing the collar to a neckline, it's best to match up the center back collar piece and the center back of the body. If you sew each side starting from the center back, your collar will always match up evenly on each side at the center front.

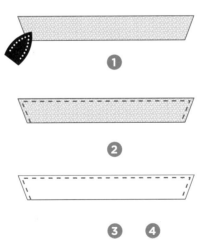

TIP:

Use a wooden point to push the corners out completely after you have turned it in step 3—you'll need help if you're working with thick wool. Another trick I like is to sew a piece of dental floss in the corner, so that when you turn it, you can pull on the floss to pull the corner out. Use very short stitches when sewing around the corner, so that when you push or pull the corner out, you won't break the seam.

TIP:

If the coat's fabric is too heavy to make a self-lined hood, I would suggest turning back the seam allowance and topstitching it so that you have a nice clean finish. You can cover the center seam with self binding.

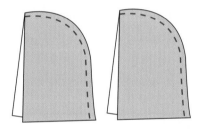

OUTER HOOD   INSIDE HOOD

①

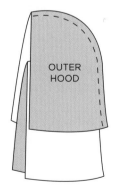

INSIDE HOOD
turned right side out

HOODS

Since you see the inside of a hood whether you're wearing it or not, it's best to line the hood. My preferred way to line a hood is with the same fabric as the garment, as opposed to lining fabric. This is called a self-lined hood. However, if you're using lining as a design element (say, a bright plaid flannel or pretty floral cotton) then it's fun to line the hood with lining, too, for an extra peek!

1. With right sides together, stitch each side of the outer hood together. Do the same for the inside hood.

2. With right sides together, stitch the outside hood to the inside hood around the front edge. Turn the pieces right side out.

3. Stitch to the garment neckline as shown in the illustration.

②

TIP:

Try making a drawstring hood by sewing a buttonhole onto each side of the hood (but not the lining!) and then topstitching around the opening, creating a tunnel. Insert cording (why not pick something decorative, like a bright color?) into one buttonhole and pull it through to the other side, using a large safety pin to help guide the way.

③

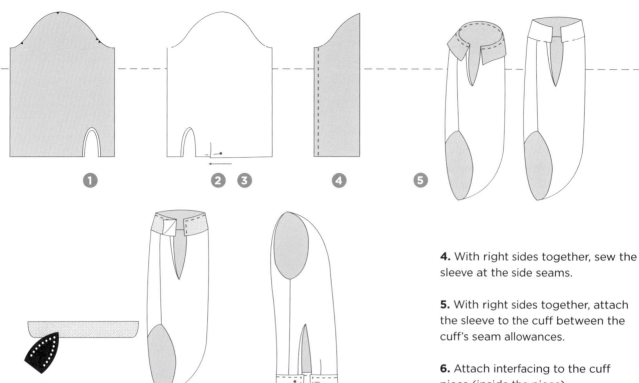

CUFFS

Cuffs are functional as well as fashionable: Fitted cuffs keep wrists warm in cold gusts of wind. They can also make a garment look more sporty and draw attention to a great pair of gloves. Here's how to sew them for some projects in this book:

1. Sew the placket piece to the sleeve opening. This is the same way you would sew a piece of bias binding to an opening.

2. Press the placket part closest to the back side seam flat, while pressing the other placket side inside the sleeve.

3. Fold the pleat, matching the markings, folding it towards the back side seam. Pin the pleat in place.

4. With right sides together, sew the sleeve at the side seams.

5. With right sides together, attach the sleeve to the cuff between the cuff's seam allowances.

6. Attach interfacing to the cuff piece (inside the piece).

7. With right sides together, sew the cuffs together around the outer edge. Turn the right side out.

8. Fold under the inside cuff's seam allowance.

9. On the right side of the cuff, topstitch around the entire cuff.

10. Attach buttons and make buttonholes, or attach whichever type of closure you prefer (you might also try snaps for an activewear look).

piece signs CONTINUED

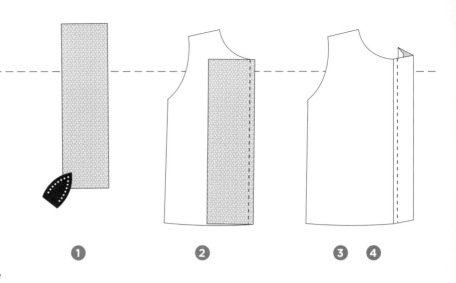

1 **2** **3** **4**

EXTENSIONS

As we went over in chapter 2, these pieces are important for the functionality of a coat. When sewing them, you'll be attaching them to the front of the garment.

1. Attach the interfacing to the wrong side of the extension.

2. With right sides together, stitch the extension to the front piece.

3. Fold back the seam allowance of the other side then fold the extension in half.

4. Topstitch the extension to the front.

TIP:

Extensions are set up in a number of ways. Sometimes a zipper is sandwiched between the extension and the front, while sometimes there is an extension on the front of the garment hiding the zipper underneath and also one inside the front protecting the zipper from pinching your clothes. I'll cover specific sewing instructions for each project in the book.

EXTRA, EXTRA: *A GUIDE TO PIECES ATTACHED TO OPENINGS*

Bottoms

Sometimes a bottom opening will have a ruffle piece attached, but for most coats and jackets, you'll just hem the bottom.

Sleeves

As with bottoms, you can add a ruffle piece if your design requires it, but most jackets and coats will use a cuff piece.

Front

Some fronts, as we've covered, will have an extension piece attached.

Armholes

Unless you're making a vest, each armhole will be finished with a sleeve, which is really another type of piece.

Necks

Usually, but not always, necks will have a collar or hood attached.

the icing on the cake
ATTACHING DETAILS

The details of a coat or jacket can really make or break the look, so be sure you take the time to attach them correctly! Here's a quick primer on sewing pockets, buttons and buttonholes, ruffles, zippers, and more.

PATCHING THINGS UP: ATTACHING POCKETS

For most of the projects in this book, we will be sewing patch pockets (attached to the outside of the garment; kangaroo pockets fall into this category) or inseam pockets (on the inside of the garment, attached along the side seam). You're always free to add or subtract these elements as you see fit. Patch pockets are fun opportunities to play with shape, texture, contrast, and trim, while inseam pockets are invisible on the outside of the garment and thus more subdued (which may be what you're after); inseam pockets make more sense for coats made of super-plush fabrics, like faux fur. Both types of pockets are relatively easy to sew. I'm not going to cover welt pockets here because they're a bit more advanced, but if you're familiar with sewing them, feel free to incorporate them into your designs.

Patch Pockets

1. Finish the hem edge of the pocket. (Kangaroo pockets will have two of these.)

2. Fold back the top hem towards the right side.

3. Stitch the length of the hem along the side seam allowances.

4. Trim the area and fold back the hem to the inside. At this point, you can topstitch the hem, if you want that design detail.

5. Fold back the seam allowance along the side and bottom edges and press.

6. Pin the pocket to the garment and stitch around the side and bottom.

KANGAROO POCKETS

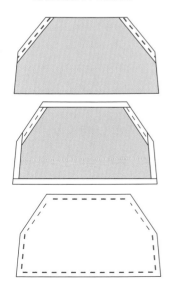

PATCH POCKETS

POCKET FLAPS

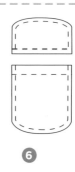

Pocket Flaps

1. Attach interfacing to the wrong sides of both pieces of the flap.

2. With right sides together, sew around the sides and bottom.

3. Trim the seam allowance if necessary.

4. Turn the piece right side out, and press. Topstitch for detail, if you prefer.

5. Finish the raw edge.

6. Lay the pocket flap piece upside down 1″ (2.5cm) above the pocket. Sew along the seam allowance.

7. Fold down the pocket flap and topstitch along the top edge.

8. Add a closure if you prefer.

Side Seam Pockets

1. With right sides together, sew the pocket front to the front of the garment at the side seam, leaving ½″ (13mm) open at the top and bottom. Do the same to attach the pocket back to the back of the garment.

2. With right sides together, sew the garment front to the back at the side seams and around the pockets.

3. Finish the pocket's seam allowance.

SIDE SEAM POCKETS

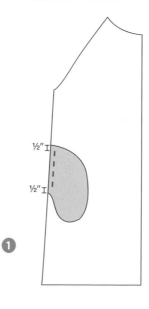

½″ ⊥

½″ ⊥

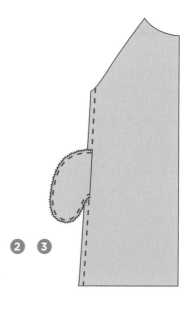

THE DOTTED LINE: *TOPSTITCHING*

Topstitching does not form seams. It is used to secure hems or other edge finishing (like the borders of pockets) and is visible on the garment—unlike seams' stitching, which is hidden to the eye. It usually involves stitching a line about ¼" (6mm) away from the seam line. Topstitching serves a function, but it can also be used for decorative purposes: You can choose contrast or metallic thread, for instance, or try a double row of stitching placed a ¼" (6mm) apart for a finish known as "double topstitching," maybe even in a thicker thread typically used for denim, for a super sporty look. Sometimes, this type of stitching is placed only ¹⁄₁₆" or ⅛" (1mm or 3mm) away from the seam line, in which case it's called edgestitching. Because this stitch is right at the seam, it's meant not to be as noticeable; you probably won't want to use decorative thread here.

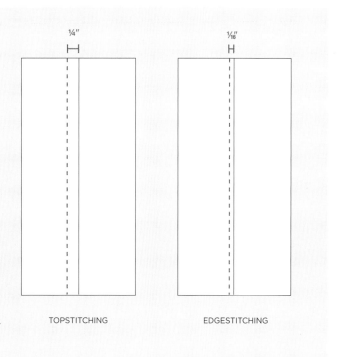

TOPSTITCHING   EDGESTITCHING

FRILL SEEKING: RUFFLES

Ruffles are really just rectangular pieces attached to openings; they get their frilly shape when you pull a basted thread through them. For such a simple and easy-to-sew piece, they pack a powerful design punch—they can really make a coat look dramatic and expensive. Why not utilize them in unexpected ways? I love the idea of a leather bomber jacket with a ruffled collar, or ruffles sandwiched between the perimeter of patch pockets and the body of the coat.

1. Fold the ruffle piece in half lengthwise with wrong sides together.

2. Sew a long basting stitch within the seam allowance—usually ¼" (6mm) from the raw edge—through both layers.

3. Pull the bobbin threads on each end of the piece and it will gather up, creating a ruffle. The more you pull, the denser the ruffle will look; be sure you create a consistent, evenly gathered look and length throughout the garment!

4. Sew this piece to your garment along the seam allowance. Remove the bobbin thread, and voilà!

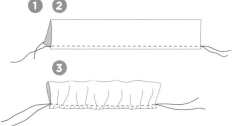

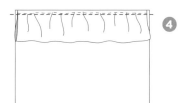

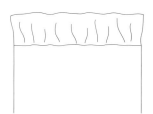

IT'S A CINCH: BELTS AND CARRIERS

Belts add sexy, slenderizing waist definition to an outerwear garment and are among the simplest sewing tasks in outerwear. Classic trench coats, for example, also sometimes have little belts on sleeves, which keep the rain off your wrists and look superchic to boot. You might try adding that detail on a different style, like a wool motorcycle jacket. Belts are threaded through belt loops or other types of carriers. Since those, like patch pockets, are attached on the outside of a garment, they're also a place to play with design. Try making a thick, long tunnel across the back of the jacket, or adding decorative topstitching to accentuate this detail.

TIP:

If you're making a two-piece belt, first sew the center back seam, and then follow the above directions for sewing a belt.

Belt

1. Fold the belt lengthwise with right sides together.

2. Stitch around all the sides, leaving about a 5″ (12.5cm) opening in the center of the belt's length.

3. Trim the corners and turn the belt right side out through the opening.

BELT

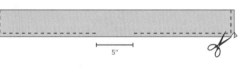

4. Fold back the seam allowance of the opening and topstitch around the entire belt.

Carrier

1. Fold the carrier piece in half lengthwise, and then fold in the ¼″ (6mm) seam allowance along each side edge.

2. Topstitch along each side of the length of the carrier.

3. Fold back the top and the bottom by ½″ (13mm), and topstitch the top and bottom to the garment.

CARRIER

BUTTONED UP: SEWING BUTTONS AND BUTTONHOLES

Buttons come in an endless array of colors, shapes, and sizes—and they even come without visible holes (a type known as shank buttons)—but they all go on essentially the same way. Give this section a read even if you've done it many times before, especially since we're working with coats and jackets: These buttons have a heavier burden. If you sew buttons on right, they'll stay on a lot longer. (But always buy a few extra, just in case....)

Buttonholes

Your sewing machine should have an automatic buttonholer; most modern versions do, so follow the instructions in your manual. Set your machine to the length that will cover your button size (the hole should be ⅛" [3mm] longer than

the button width). Make sure that the placket where you're making holes has interfacing attached to make the fabric sturdier; otherwise the holes may cause the surrounding area to pucker up. Measure the button layout extremely

carefully, and mark the locations first using your clear ruler, making sure the buttonholes are at even intervals and centered perfectly. Start with the bottom button first—mistakes won't be as obvious there. Place the needle at the top of where the opening will be, and the machine will work its way down. Then fold the fabric and gently snip the hole open, finish with fray sealant or even clear nail polish, and you're good to go!

Attaching Buttons

If a button is sewn on too tightly, it won't have any room to move. Especially when it comes to coats, which tend to use heavy fabric and be harder to close, you need to give it some space. For most buttons, you'll need to create a shank—which is essentially a stem of wrapped thread—so that the button can do its job without snapping off. Some buttons come with shanks already. Shank buttons will have a little protruding loop or stem on the back with a hole that allows the button to move freely. If you're using this kind of button, you might be able to skip step 3. But if your fabric is thick faux fur, for instance, the button will still need to stand away from the placket enough so that it can move around.

A good rule of thumb is to make sure that the shank (whether it's your thread shank, the button shank, or a combination of both) is longer than the buttonhole placket is thick.

Some sewers like to use special button thread, but I prefer to save money and double up my regular thread instead. But, jackets and coats require special attention: If the fabric you're using for a coat is super-thick and the button is big and heavy, try doubling it up twice, or using embroidery thread. It all depends on how much stress will be on the button. If your coat uses super-dense felt and heavy metal buttons, you'd better make it thick!

1. Starting from underneath, pierce the surface of the placket with the threaded needle. Make a few stitches through the placket to secure the thread in place.

2. Place two crossed straight pins where the button will lie to create some space between the button and the garment. Then place the button on top of the pins, and stitch through the holes of the button and down through the fabric and back up through the buttons holes again at least three or four times.

3. Remove the pins. Wind the thread around the threads that are in between the button and the fabric a few times, enough so that the button can easily slip through the buttonhole. This will create a shank for added strength and flexibility.

4. Bring the thread through to the wrong side of the fabric. Stitch a few times to secure it, then knot the loose threads (more than once, since we're working with jackets and coats) and clip them off.

TEETH TIME: ZIPPERS

To make a jacket with a zipper front, you must use a separating zipper. This type of zipper opens at the top and bottom, as opposed to the kind used for pants or dresses. Make sure you ask for one at the fabric store, or you're likely to get the wrong kind—and you don't want to find yourself unable to squeeze into your beautiful, brand-new skintight biker jacket because it doesn't open at the bottom!

1. Finish the front edges of the front of the garment.

2. With right sides together, baste the front pieces of the garment together.

3. Press the front pieces open.

4. Pin the zipper, face down, to the seam allowances, centering the zipper teeth on the basted seam line.

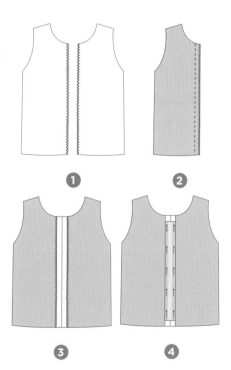

I OF THE NEEDLE: *QUICK TIPS FOR THREADING RIGHT*

I hate hand-stitching, but it's the only way to attach buttons. Luckily, it's a pretty simple process. To save yourself the effort of having to stitch through the button's holes many times, it's easiest to double-thread your needle, creating a thicker and stronger thread and cutting your workload in half.

1. Cut a length of thread. If you're not sure how much you need, try about 18" (45.5cm).

2. Fold the thread in half and thread the folded tip through the eye of the needle (you might want to use a larger-eyed needle and a threader for help).

3. Knot the loose ends. I like to knot them at least twice to make sure that the knot is big enough. If it's not, it may slip right through the fabric! If you have a hard time seeing the knot, that usually means you should keep knotting.

5. Turn the garment over to the face side and topstitch ¼" (6mm) from each side of the basted seam, starting from the bottom.

6. Remove the basting stitches.

⑤   **⑥**

THE HEAT IS ON: *PRESSING*

You must, must, MUST press each seam open after you sew it. Why? The pieces won't lie fully flat until you do, and once a seam is joined to another seam, it's not going to behave any differently. If you don't press it first to fully open it up, you won't be able to do so correctly after it's joined, and it may create bunching or asymmetry in the garment. Some pieces, like collars, must be pressed first, too, because you'll need to topstitch them before you attach them to the garment's body. Here's how to be an iron woman:

- Always use a press cloth to protect the fabric from getting damaged by the heat, unless you're working with linen or cotton (which are not so heat sensitive).
- Always press on the wrong side of the fabric. Heat can alter the surface of the fabric, causing it to shine or fade.
- Iron in the direction of grain of the fabric that is parallel to the selvage edge so that the fabric doesn't stretch out. Be gentle.
- To avoid steam circles from the iron, use a nonsteam iron and spray water directly onto the fabric.
- Place a piece of fabric under the garment so that the heat is conducted better.
- Use a piece of fabric to cover small pieces with stitching, like cuffs, collars, and plackets, so that you don't crush the seams and create weird little wrinkles in the process.

TIP:

When attaching a facing or a lining to the zipper's seam allowance, just fold back the seam allowance of the facing or lining and hand-stitch it to the zipper tape.

TIP:

Start the zipper a ¼" (6mm) down from the top edge seam allowance: If your seam allowance is ¼" (6mm), then the top stop of the zipper should be placed ½" (13mm) down from the top raw edge. Depending on the style of your jacket or coat, the zipper will stop at different places. Generally, if you want it to end at the bottom edge of your garment, then the zipper teeth should be placed ¼" (6mm) above the hem or bottom-edge seam allowance. Measure the area where the zipper will go and buy a zipper that size. You can also buy a longer zipper and have it cut it down to size, and a stopper added to the end, at a notions store.

CHAPTER 4

THE FITTED JACKET

OUTERWEAR DOESN'T HAVE TO BE BULKY—IN FACT, IT CAN BE A GREAT WAY TO show off (or enhance) your shape! This fitted, waist-length jacket pattern is a great template to make all sorts of casual to dressy jackets. The princess seams contour the bust and nip the waist, making this a great fit or all shapes—and creating an hourglass look for those who want more curves.

The projects in this chapter run the gamut from sweet and girly to tough and sleek, but they all take a curved-seam construction as their point of departure. This extra seam in the front does require extra steps to sew, and it is a curved seam—not the easiest kind to deal with—but it really helps coats and jackets to follow the bustline. And as you'll see, a fitted jacket or coat doesn't always mean shrunken. Switching up the fabrics, trims, and pattern details can really alter the character of the pattern, whether you're in the mood for a silky kimono-style unlined wrap or a stiff schoolgirl-plaid peacoat. I've packed this chapter full of ideas for you, but don't let that stop you from dreaming up your own unique creation!

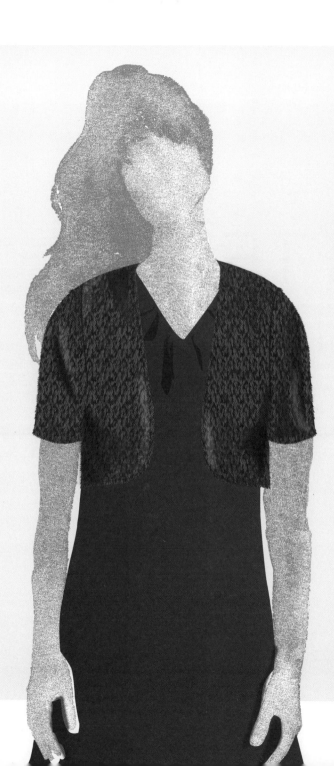

baby bolero

Sometimes faux fur can be a bit much, but it's nice in small doses. This sweet little bolero is cropped at the bust and has cap sleeves, so it's the perfect format for some luxe, shaggy fabric. It makes a cool cover-up for an evening dress—whether you're going Kate Moss glam (say, a chiffon gown) or minimal (like a wool-jersey turtleneck dress). It adds dimension and texture to everyday tops and jeans—and it keeps your shoulders warm!

supplies

1 yard (91cm) brown faux fur
1 yard (91cm) brown lining

TRY THESE TOO!
Chic: Chocolate wool cashmere
Holiday: Black silk velvet with red lining
Preppy: Khaki cotton twill with lime
    green piping around the neckline

pattern adjustments

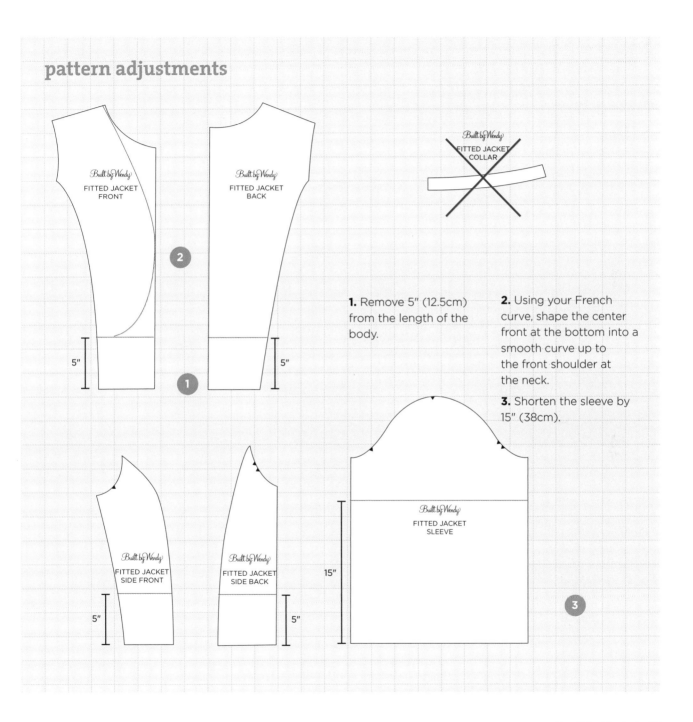

Built by Wendy
FITTED JACKET
FRONT

Built by Wendy
FITTED JACKET
BACK

Built by Wendy
FITTED JACKET
COLLAR

Built by Wendy
FITTED JACKET
SIDE FRONT

Built by Wendy
FITTED JACKET
SIDE BACK

Built by Wendy
FITTED JACKET
SLEEVE

5″

5″

5″

5″

15″

1. Remove 5″ (12.5cm) from the length of the body.

2. Using your French curve, shape the center front at the bottom into a smooth curve up to the front shoulder at the neck.

3. Shorten the sleeve by 15″ (38cm).

pattern adjustments

4. Add the seam allowances.

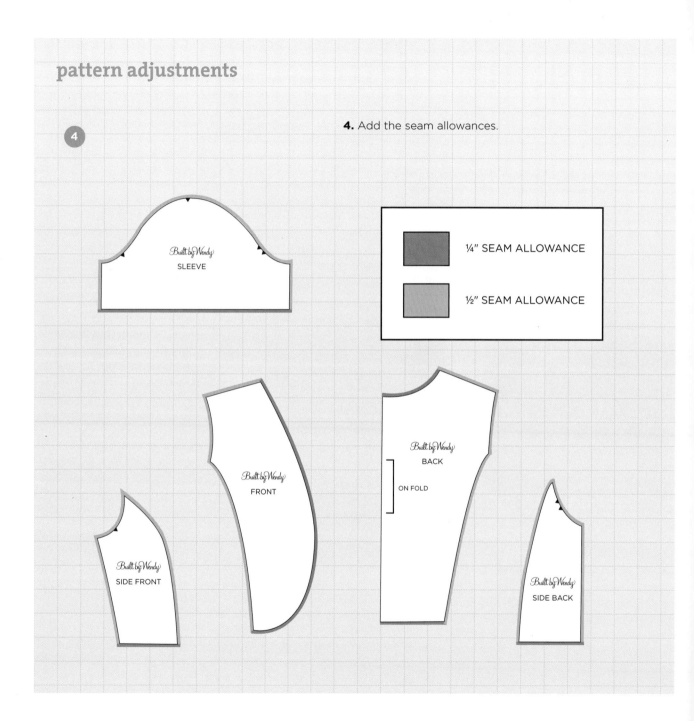

¼" SEAM ALLOWANCE

½" SEAM ALLOWANCE

Built by Wendy
SLEEVE

Built by Wendy
FRONT

Built by Wendy
BACK

ON FOLD

Built by Wendy
SIDE FRONT

Built by Wendy
SIDE BACK

cutting

Self 44" (112cm)

BACK — *Built by Wendy* — ON FOLD

FRONT — *Built by Wendy*

SIDE BACK — *Built by Wendy*

SLEEVE — *Built by Wendy*

SIDE FRONT — *Built by Wendy*

FOLD

Lining 44" (112cm)

BACK — *Built by Wendy* — ON FOLD

FRONT — *Built by Wendy*

SIDE BACK — *Built by Wendy*

SLEEVE — *Built by Wendy*

SIDE FRONT — *Built by Wendy*

FOLD

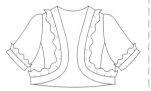

sewing

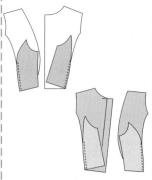

1. With right sides together, sew the front side pieces to the front, and the back side pieces to the back. Do the same for the lining.

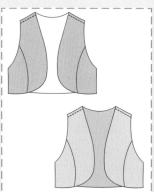

2. With right sides together, sew the front to the back at the shoulders. Do the same for the lining.

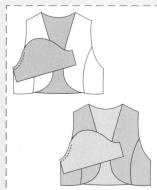

3. With right sides together, sew the sleeves to the armholes. Do the same for the lining.

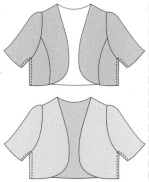

4. With right sides together, sew the front to the back at the side seams from the bottom opening to the sleeve opening. Do the same for the lining.

5. With right sides together, sew the lining to the body, leaving 5" (12.5cm) open in the center back. Turn the body right side out through this opening and slip the sleeve lining into the sleeves.

6. Hand-stitch the sleeve hem to the sleeve lining.

7. Hand-stitch the back opening closed.

pretty babydoll

This cotton jacket has a romantic, gamine silhouette that makes you feel dressed up the instant you throw it on. The gathered empire waist is an easy, flattering, flaw-hiding shape all figures can wear. The wide sixties-style neckline gives it a delicate feeling, as does the charming ribbon-front closure. Rock it with a wide headband and some false eyelashes to maximize the flirt factor.

supplies

1½ yards (1.4m) red medium-weight cotton

3 yards (2.7m) burgundy cotton ribbon

½ yard (46cm) black fusible interfacing

TRY THESE TOO!

Chic: Beige wool felt with horn toggles

Party: Blue velvet with silk frogs

Beach: White cotton terry cloth

pattern adjustments

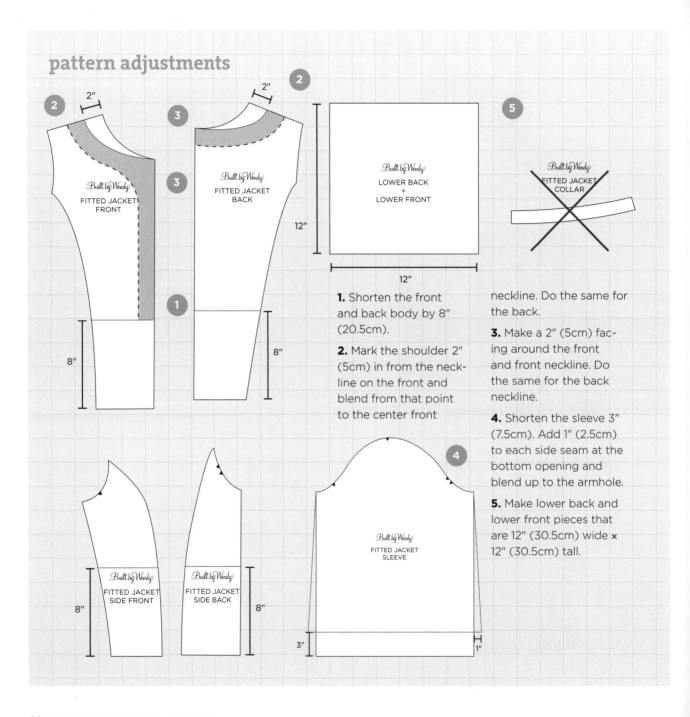

FITTED JACKET FRONT — 2", 8"

FITTED JACKET BACK — 2", 8"

LOWER BACK + LOWER FRONT — 12", 12"

FITTED JACKET COLLAR

FITTED JACKET SIDE FRONT — 8"

FITTED JACKET SIDE BACK — 8"

FITTED JACKET SLEEVE — 3", 1"

1. Shorten the front and back body by 8" (20.5cm).

2. Mark the shoulder 2" (5cm) in from the neckline on the front and blend from that point to the center front neckline. Do the same for the back.

3. Make a 2" (5cm) facing around the front and front neckline. Do the same for the back neckline.

4. Shorten the sleeve 3" (7.5cm). Add 1" (2.5cm) to each side seam at the bottom opening and blend up to the armhole.

5. Make lower back and lower front pieces that are 12" (30.5cm) wide × 12" (30.5cm) tall.

pattern adjustments

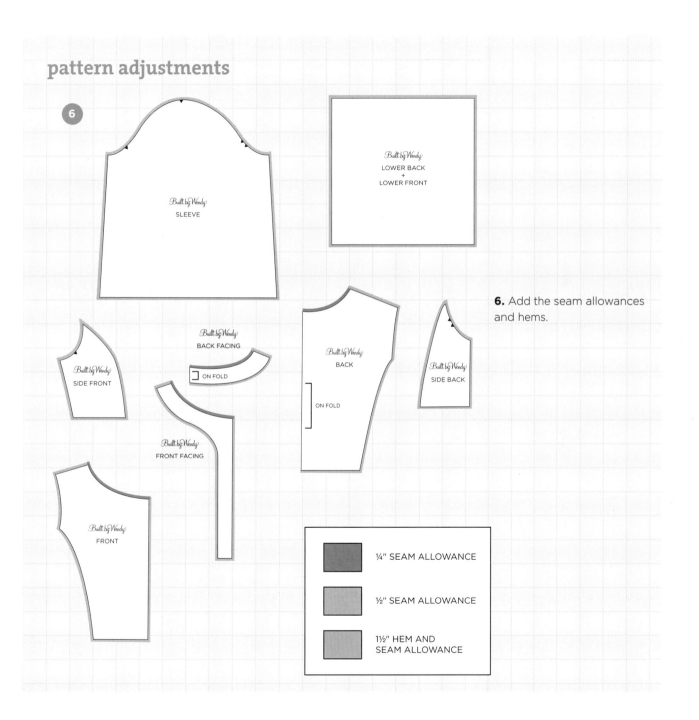

6. Add the seam allowances and hems.

SLEEVE

LOWER BACK + LOWER FRONT

BACK FACING

ON FOLD

SIDE FRONT

FRONT FACING

BACK

ON FOLD

SIDE BACK

FRONT

¼" SEAM ALLOWANCE

½" SEAM ALLOWANCE

1½" HEM AND SEAM ALLOWANCE

cutting

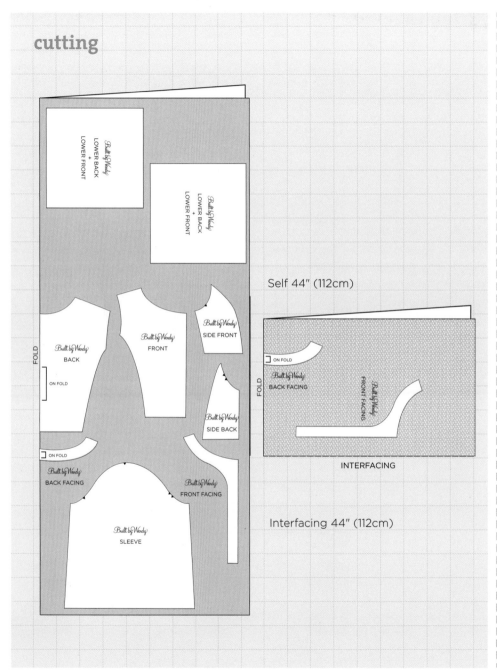

LOWER BACK + LOWER FRONT

LOWER BACK + LOWER FRONT

Built by Wendy

Self 44" (112cm)

FOLD

Built by Wendy
BACK

ON FOLD

Built by Wendy
FRONT

Built by Wendy
SIDE FRONT

Built by Wendy
SIDE BACK

ON FOLD

Built by Wendy
BACK FACING

Built by Wendy
FRONT FACING

Built by Wendy
SLEEVE

ON FOLD
Built by Wendy
BACK FACING

FOLD

Built by Wendy
FRONT FACING

INTERFACING

Interfacing 44" (112cm)

Little Red Riding Hood

Why not try making this coat in red wool or canvas? Simply add several inches (5cm–10cm) to the length so that it hits your frame the way it's shown here, and leave the sleeves and neckline untouched from the sloper. Add the hood from the basic jacket pattern (chapter 5). Finish with some cute toggles of rope and horn—and a sweater and sweet ballet flats!

sewing

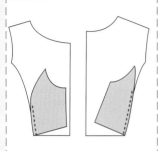

1. With right sides together, sew the front side pieces to the front pieces. Sew the back side pieces to the back.

2. With right sides together, sew the front to the back at the shoulders.

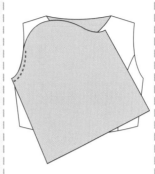

3. With right sides together, sew the sleeves to the armholes.

4. With right sides together, sew the front to the back at the side seams from the bottom opening up to the sleeve opening.

5. Fold back the sleeve hem and topstitch it down.

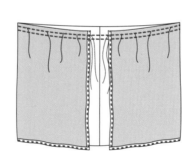

6. With right sides together sew the lower backs together, and then sew the lower backs to the lower fronts at the side seams. Fold back the hem and the front edge of the bottom piece, and topstitch them down. Gather the top edge.

sewing

7. With right sides together, sew the bottom piece to the bodice, leaving a ½″ (13mm) seam allowance at the center front.

8. Attach the interfacing to the facings. With right sides together, sew the front facing to the back facing at the shoulders.

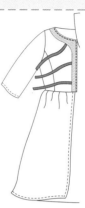

9. Pin a 15″ (38cm) length of the ribbon to each of the three points marked on each side of the front pieces. Place the three ribbons equally between the neckline and the waistline.

10. With right sides together, sew the facing to the neckline and the front, sandwiching the ribbon ties. Understitch the facing to the body and secure at the shoulder and bottom piece points.

that's a wrap

This linen jacket has an asymmetrical wrap front and ties for a chic, offbeat Japanese feeling. In indigo ikat print, it makes a totally fresh alternative to a jean jacket. You could also make it in basic black linen to wear over slouchy cropped pants for an arty Yohji Yamamoto look. It's easy to make, but it looks expensive—always a bonus, in my book!

supplies

1½ yards (1.4m) indigo ikat print cotton
½ yard (46cm) black fusible interfacing
2 yards (1.8m) indigo ribbon

TRY THESE TOO!
Basic: Cotton canvas in every color
Evening: Slouchy black satin
*Nautical: Green cotton twill with ribbon
    stripes down the front and a toggle
    closure*

pattern adjustments

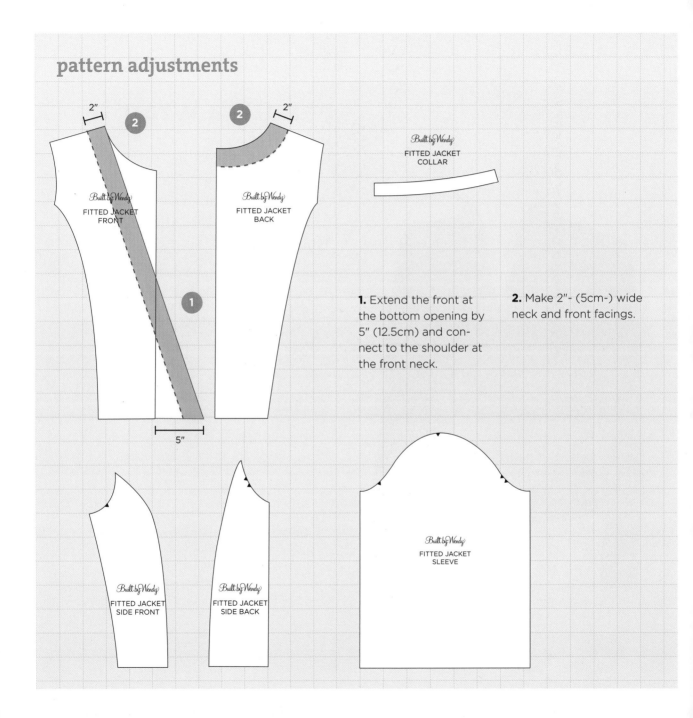

1. Extend the front at the bottom opening by 5″ (12.5cm) and connect to the shoulder at the front neck.

2. Make 2″- (5cm-) wide neck and front facings.

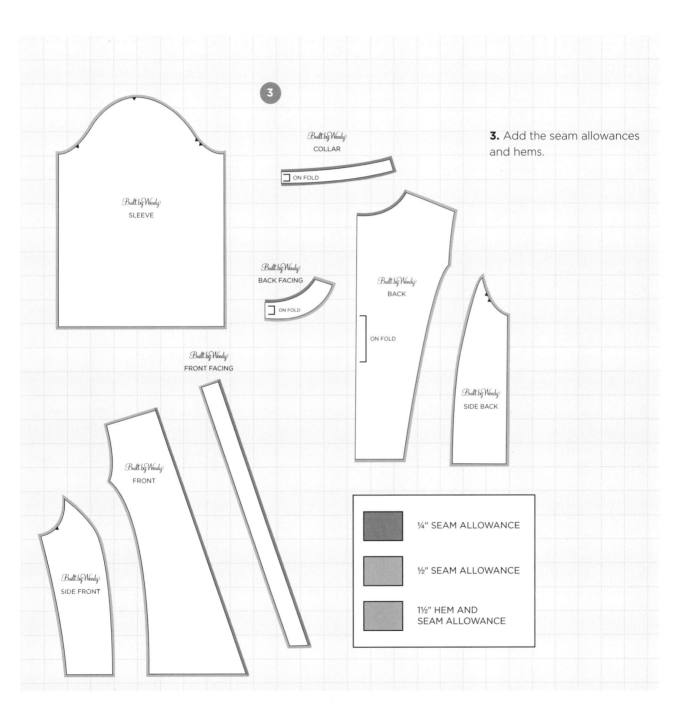

Built by Wendy
COLLAR

ON FOLD

3. Add the seam allowances and hems.

Built by Wendy
SLEEVE

Built by Wendy
BACK FACING

ON FOLD

Built by Wendy
BACK

ON FOLD

Built by Wendy
FRONT FACING

Built by Wendy
SIDE BACK

Built by Wendy
FRONT

Built by Wendy
SIDE FRONT

	¼" SEAM ALLOWANCE
	½" SEAM ALLOWANCE
	1½" HEM AND SEAM ALLOWANCE

cutting

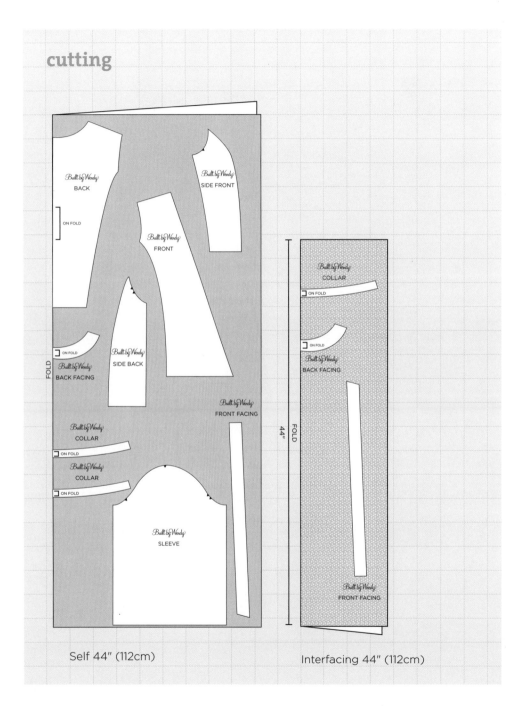

Self 44" (112cm)

Interfacing 44" (112cm)

Built by Wendy
BACK

ON FOLD

Built by Wendy
SIDE FRONT

Built by Wendy
FRONT

FOLD

ON FOLD

Built by Wendy
BACK FACING

Built by Wendy
SIDE BACK

Built by Wendy
FRONT FACING

Built by Wendy
COLLAR

ON FOLD

Built by Wendy
COLLAR

ON FOLD

Built by Wendy
SLEEVE

Built by Wendy
COLLAR

ON FOLD

FOLD

44"

Built by Wendy
BACK FACING

ON FOLD

Built by Wendy
FRONT FACING

The New Wave Jacket

Want further evidence that by changing fabric and trims, you can completely change a jacket? Look no further than this spin on the wrap jacket pattern, here in black wool felt with an exposed metal zipper inserted into the asymmetrical front in lieu of ties. Make a facing in neon pink fabric for a flash of bold color. Add matching lipstick, if you dare!

sewing

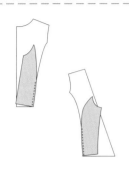

1. With right sides together, sew the front side pieces to the front pieces. Sew the back side pieces to the back.

2. With right sides together, sew the fronts to the back at the shoulders.

3. With right sides together, sew the sleeves to the armholes.

4. With right sides together, sandwich two 15″ (38cm) ribbons placed 4″ (10cm) apart inside the left-hand side seam. (For placement of the ribbons I would try on the jacket and mark where you would like the ties; it's probably best near the bottom and under the bust.) Sew the front to the back at the side seams from the bottom opening to the sleeve opening.

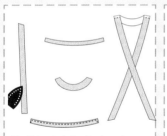

5. Attach interfacing to the collar and the facings. With right sides together, sew the front to the back facing at the shoulders.

6. With right sides together, sew collar pieces together around the sides and the top edge. Turn the collar right side out.

7. With right sides together, sew the collar to the neckline, matching up the pieces at the center back.

8. Pin two 15″ (38cm) lengths of ribbon to the front at the opening edge, matching up their placement with the side seam ribbons.

9. With right sides together, sew the facing to the neck-line, front, and bottom opening, sandwiching the front ties in between the seam. Understitch and secure at the shoulder.

10. Hem the sleeve and bottom openings.

go speed racer!

Sleek, body-conscious, and sportswear-inspired, this leatherette jacket gets its tough vibe from metal eyelet-and-snap details (kind of like a grown-up version of "BeDazzling") that are added to external armhole facings. It's the ultimate urban-cool companion to your favorite skinny jeans, and can also be the perfect foil to de-girlify a floaty dress (just add boots or oxfords).

supplies

2 yards (1.8m) black leatherette
1 yard (91cm) black fusible interfacing
20 size 8mm silver eyelets
7 size 24 silver snaps
Snap and grommet fastener

TRY THESE TOO!
Chic: Olive Ultrasuede with oversized buttons
Rustic: Brown wool tweed with gold buckle closures
Preppy: Red cotton twill with a madras lining

pattern adjustments

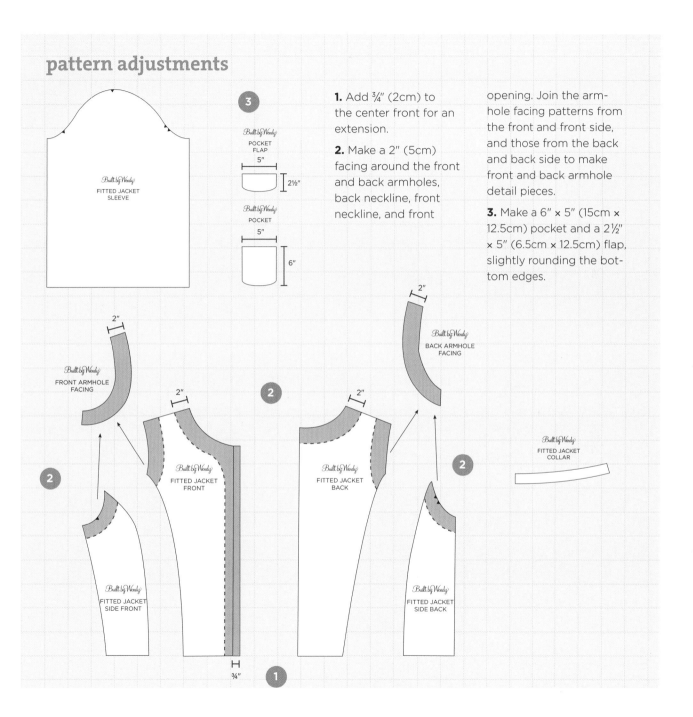

1. Add ¾″ (2cm) to the center front for an extension.

2. Make a 2″ (5cm) facing around the front and back armholes, back neckline, front neckline, and front opening. Join the armhole facing patterns from the front and front side, and those from the back and back side to make front and back armhole detail pieces.

3. Make a 6″ × 5″ (15cm × 12.5cm) pocket and a 2½″ × 5″ (6.5cm × 12.5cm) flap, slightly rounding the bottom edges.

POCKET FLAP
5″
2½″

POCKET
5″
6″

FITTED JACKET SLEEVE

FRONT ARMHOLE FACING
2″

BACK ARMHOLE FACING
2″

FITTED JACKET FRONT
2″

FITTED JACKET BACK
2″

FITTED JACKET COLLAR

FITTED JACKET SIDE FRONT

FITTED JACKET SIDE BACK

¾″

pattern adjustments

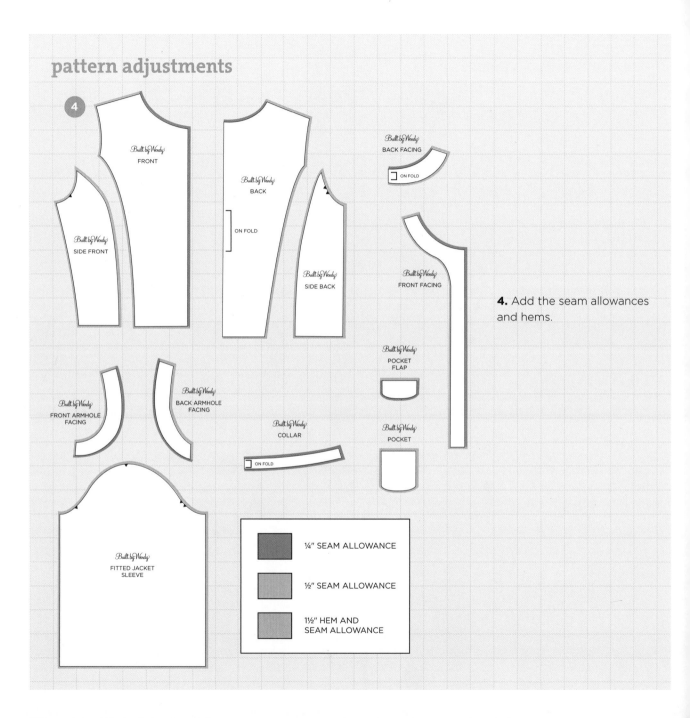

4

Built by Wendy
FRONT

Built by Wendy
SIDE FRONT

Built by Wendy
BACK

ON FOLD

Built by Wendy
SIDE BACK

Built by Wendy
BACK FACING

ON FOLD

Built by Wendy
FRONT FACING

4. Add the seam allowances and hems.

Built by Wendy
POCKET
FLAP

Built by Wendy
FRONT ARMHOLE
FACING

Built by Wendy
BACK ARMHOLE
FACING

Built by Wendy
COLLAR

ON FOLD

Built by Wendy
POCKET

Built by Wendy
FITTED JACKET
SLEEVE

¼" SEAM ALLOWANCE

½" SEAM ALLOWANCE

1½" HEM AND
SEAM ALLOWANCE

cutting

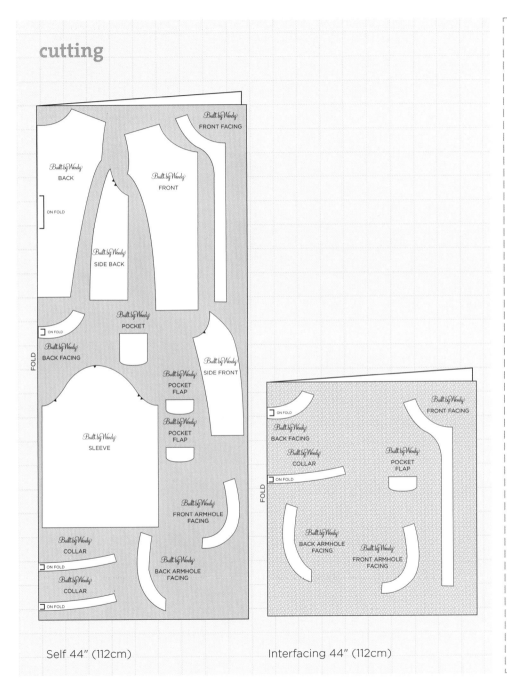

Self 44" (112cm)

Interfacing 44" (112cm)

Pattern pieces labeled "Built by Wendy":
BACK · FRONT · FRONT FACING · SIDE BACK · POCKET · BACK FACING · SIDE FRONT · POCKET FLAP · SLEEVE · FRONT ARMHOLE FACING · COLLAR · BACK ARMHOLE FACING · COLLAR

Interfacing pieces: FRONT FACING · BACK FACING · COLLAR · POCKET FLAP · BACK ARMHOLE FACING · FRONT ARMHOLE FACING

ALTERNATIVE

The Emperor's New Jacket

The simple shape of this jacket lends itself well to dressier interpretations that really show off the fabric, like this classic Asian-inspired topper. To make it, simply leave off the armhole detail facings and grommets, and use a simple red Chinese jacquard silk for the body. Use sew-on snaps inside for a clean finish. I love the way this looks with boyfriend jeans, a tee, and some killer platforms.

sewing

1. With right sides together, sew the front side pieces to the front pieces. Sew the back side pieces to the back.

2. With right sides together, sew the front to the back at the shoulders.

3. Attach interfacing to the collar, pocket flaps, facings, and armhole details.

4. With right sides together, sew the front and back armhole details together at the shoulder and sew the front facing to the back facing at the shoulders.

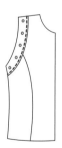

5. Attach eyelets to the armhole detail facings as shown about 1″ (2.5cm) apart, evenly spaced, or in any pattern you like. Fold the hem on the inner edges of the armhole detail pieces, pin them to the body, and edge-stitch them down. Pin the outer edges to the armholes.

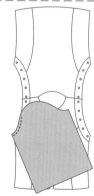

6. With right sides together, sew the sleeves to the armholes, sandwiching the armhole detail piece.

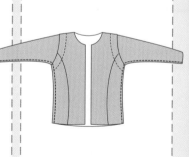

7. With right sides together, sew the front to the back at the side seams from the bottom opening to the sleeve opening.

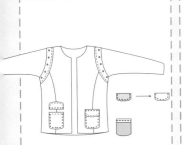

8. Sew the pocket flaps. Topstitch the pockets and flaps to the body.

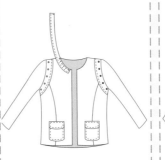

9. With right sides together, sew the collar pieces together around the sides and the top edge. Turn it right side out and topstitch it.

10. With right sides together, sew the collar to the neckline.

11. With right sides together, sew the facing to the neckline, the front, and bottom opening. Turn right side out, topstitch it, and secure it to the shoulder seams.

12. Fold back the bottom opening hem and topstitch.

13. Fold back the sleeve opening hem and topstitch.

14. Attach snaps onto the front and pocket flaps, placing the snaps first at the top and bottom, then at the center of the front. Then place the other two snaps equally between the bottom and center and the center and top. Center the pocket flap snaps on the flap so that there is a ½" (13mm) space between the snap's bottom edge and the pocket flap's bottom edge.

la parisienne

Whipped up in bouclé wool shot through with shimmering Lurex, this jacket is a chic classic in the vein of the Chanel version we all know and love. It takes a basic outfit up a notch and works flawlessly in day or evening situations, whether with jeans or a crisp pencil skirt and heels. It's also totally appropriate for every age group—try making one for your mom, too!

supplies

1½ yards (1.4m) gray-and-black flecked wool bouclé

1½ yards (1.4m) black lining

1 yard (91cm) black fusible interfacing

10" (25.5cm) of ¼"- (6mm-) wide black satin ribbon

TRY THESE TOO!

Basic: Black silk crepe with a striped lining

Modern Vintage: Medium blue denim

Preppy: Beige corduroy with a leatherette belt

pattern adjustments

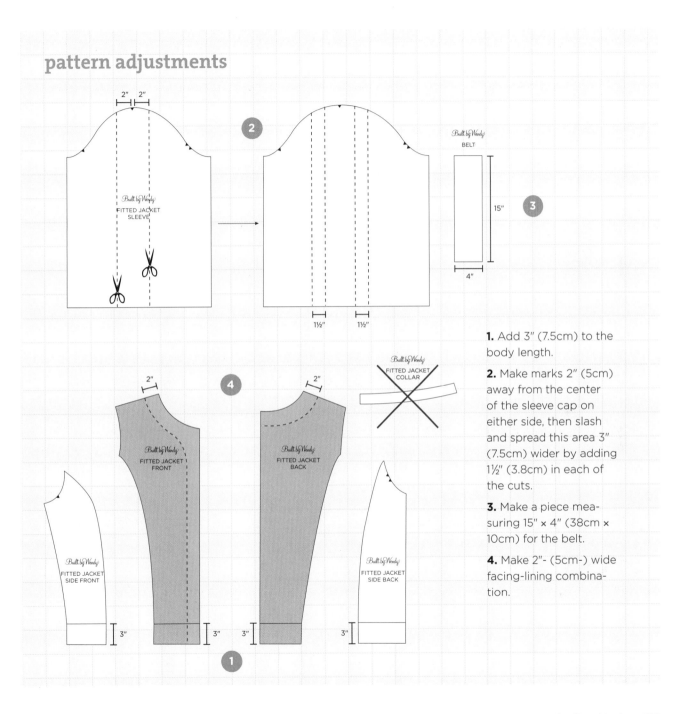

1. Add 3″ (7.5cm) to the body length.

2. Make marks 2″ (5cm) away from the center of the sleeve cap on either side, then slash and spread this area 3″ (7.5cm) wider by adding 1½″ (3.8cm) in each of the cuts.

3. Make a piece measuring 15″ × 4″ (38cm × 10cm) for the belt.

4. Make 2″- (5cm-) wide facing-lining combination.

pattern adjustments

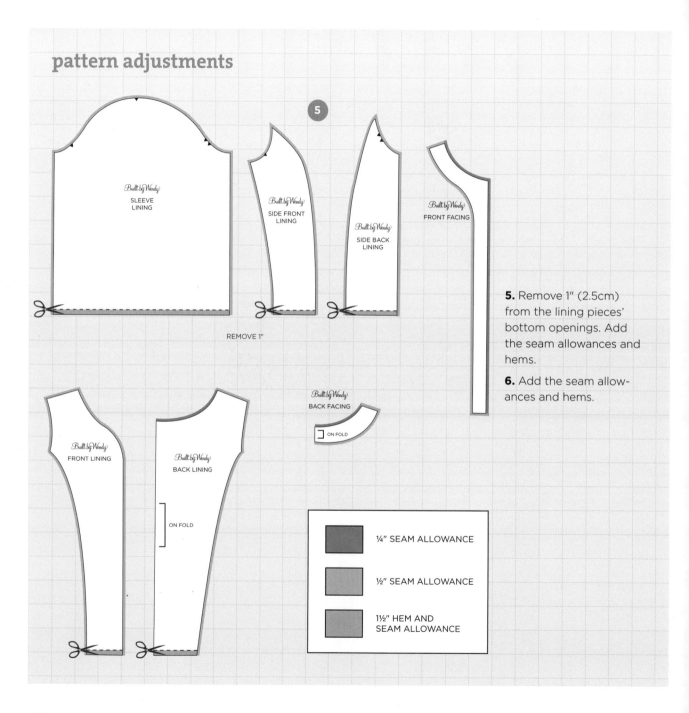

Built by Wendy
SLEEVE LINING

Built by Wendy
SIDE FRONT LINING

Built by Wendy
SIDE BACK LINING

Built by Wendy
FRONT FACING

REMOVE 1"

Built by Wendy
FRONT LINING

Built by Wendy
BACK LINING

ON FOLD

Built by Wendy
BACK FACING

ON FOLD

5. Remove 1" (2.5cm) from the lining pieces' bottom openings. Add the seam allowances and hems.

6. Add the seam allowances and hems.

¼" SEAM ALLOWANCE

½" SEAM ALLOWANCE

1½" HEM AND SEAM ALLOWANCE

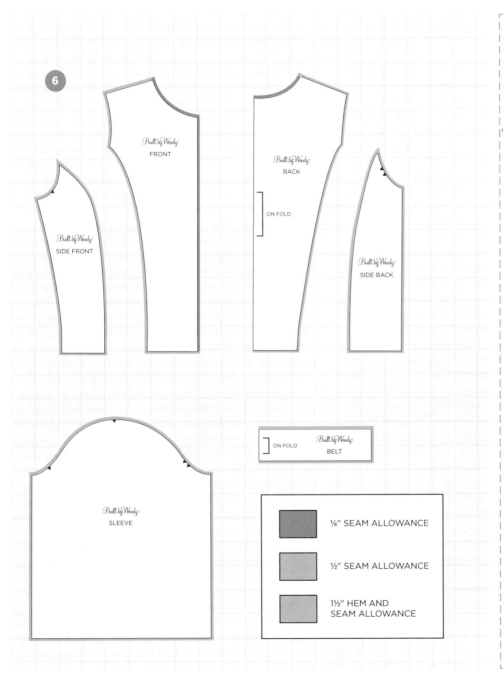

6

Built by Wendy
FRONT

Built by Wendy
SIDE FRONT

Built by Wendy
BACK

ON FOLD

Built by Wendy
SIDE BACK

Built by Wendy
SLEEVE

ON FOLD   *Built by Wendy*
BELT

¼" SEAM ALLOWANCE

½" SEAM ALLOWANCE

1½" HEM AND
SEAM ALLOWANCE

The Garden Party Jacket

Instead of adding to the length of the jacket, try shortening the original pattern by 2″ (5cm) so that it's really cropped at your natural waist for a chic, dressy, figure-defining look. If you make it in a brightly colored silk or cotton and add some floral appliqués on the chest, you'll have a surefire conversation starter! This variation would also look cute in a big, bright eighties floral print over a pencil skirt.

cutting

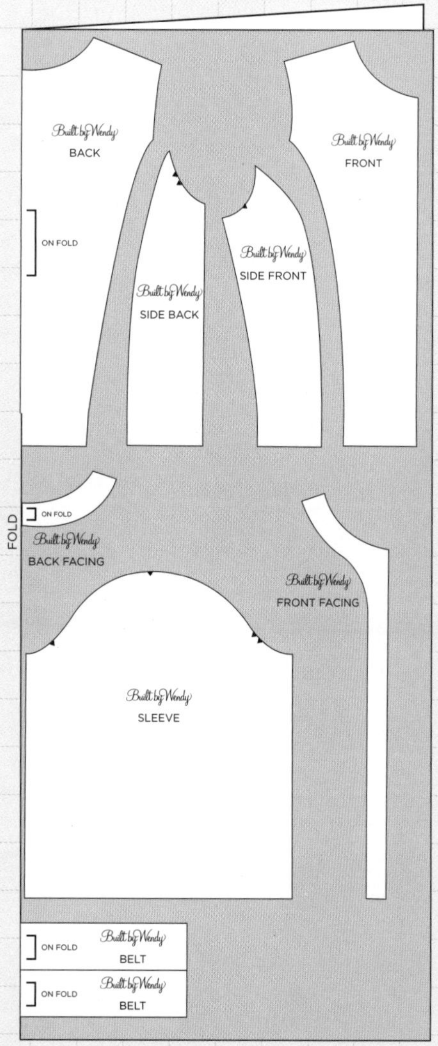

Self 44" (112cm)

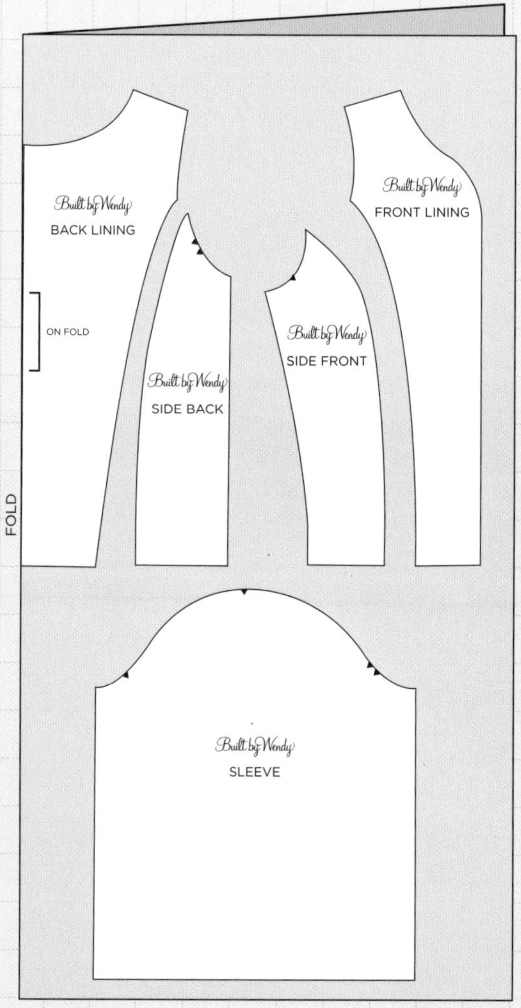

Pattern pieces shown:
- Built by Wendy — BACK
- Built by Wendy — FRONT
- Built by Wendy — SIDE BACK
- Built by Wendy — SIDE FRONT
- Built by Wendy — BACK FACING
- Built by Wendy — FRONT FACING
- Built by Wendy — SLEEVE
- Built by Wendy — BELT
- Built by Wendy — BELT
- ON FOLD / FOLD markings

Lining 44" (112cm)

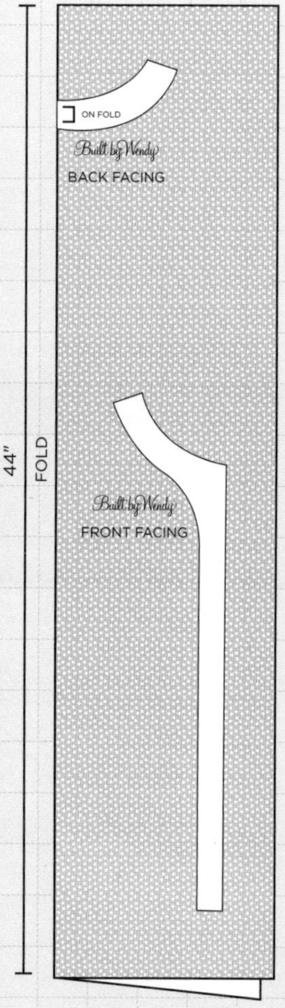

Pattern pieces shown:
- Built by Wendy — BACK LINING
- Built by Wendy — FRONT LINING
- Built by Wendy — SIDE BACK
- Built by Wendy — SIDE FRONT
- Built by Wendy — SLEEVE
- ON FOLD / FOLD markings

Interfacing 44" (112cm)

Pattern pieces shown:
- Built by Wendy — BACK FACING
- Built by Wendy — FRONT FACING
- ON FOLD / FOLD / 44" markings

sewing

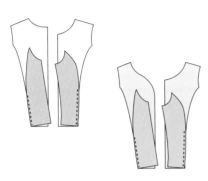

1. With right sides together, sew the front side pieces to the front pieces. Sew the side pieces to the back. Do the same for the lining.

2. With right sides together, sew the front to the back at the shoulders. Do the same for the lining.

3. Baste and gather each sleeve cap, and then, with right sides together, sew the sleeves to the armholes. Do the same for the lining.

4. With right sides together, sew the front to the back at the side seams from the bottom opening to the sleeve opening. Do the same for the lining. Hem the lining's bottom opening.

sewing

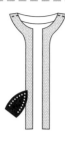

5. Attach interfacing to the facing pieces. With right sides together, sew the front facing to the back facing at the shoulders.

6. With right sides together, sew the lining to the facing around the neckline and fronts.

7. With right sides together, sew the garment to the facing around the neckline and fronts. Sew the front facing's bottom along the width of the hem.

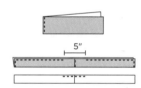

8. Turn the garment right side out, then fold up the hem of the bottom opening and hand-stitch the lining's bottom opening to the garment hem.

9. Fold back the sleeve opening and sleeve lining's opening hems and hand-stitch them together.

10. Hand-stitch a 2½" (6.5cm) length of ribbon to each side seam at the waist where you want the belt to go.

11. With right sides together, sew two short ends of the belt pieces together. Fold belt in half lengthwise, right sides together, and stitch around the length, leaving 5" (12.5cm) open. Turn belt right side out through the opening. Hand-stitch opening shut. Put belt through the loops on the side seams and tie in a bow.

the perfect peacoat

No self-respecting style-phile should be without a chic, classic peacoat. And no peacoat will fit you better than one you design and tailor for yourself! This timeless coat was originally a men's style, so I've updated it with a stand-up collar. Big anchor buttons lend a touch of whimsy without ruining the overall clean look. It's the ultimate winter staple!

supplies

2 yards (1.8m) navy wool felt

2 yards (1.8m) navy lining

1 yard (91cm) black fusible interfacing

6 size 45 ligne navy anchor buttons

TRY THESE TOO!

Chic: White mohair with flat buttons

Goth: Burgundy velvet with antique Victorian buttons

Preppy: Red tartan

pattern adjustments

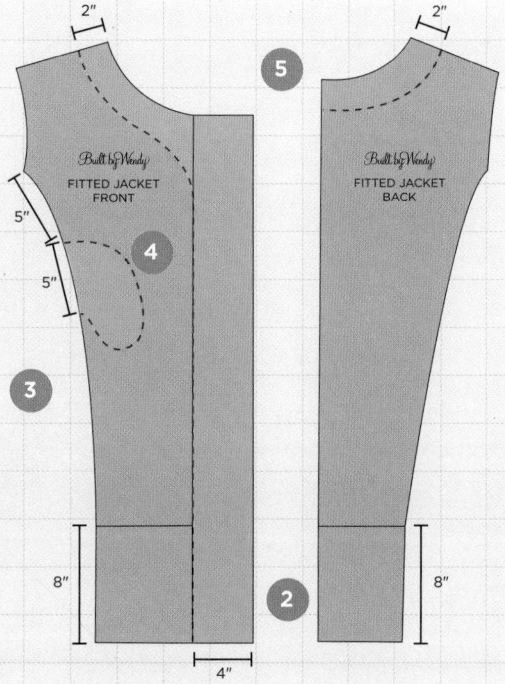

2"

2"

5

2"

FITTED JACKET FRONT
Built by Wendy

FITTED JACKET BACK
Built by Wendy

5"

5"

4

3

8"

2

8"

4"

1. Add 8" (20.5cm) to the body length.

2. Add 4" (10cm) to the center front for the extension.

3. Make a small notch along the front seams 5" (12.5cm) down from

the top, and another one 5" (12.5cm) down from there.

4. Make an inseam pocket that will open between the notches.

5. Make a 2"- (5cm-) wide facing and lining com bination, starting at the 2" (5cm) mark at the shoulders, then blending to the 4" (10cm) width of the front extension. Do the same for the back neckline.

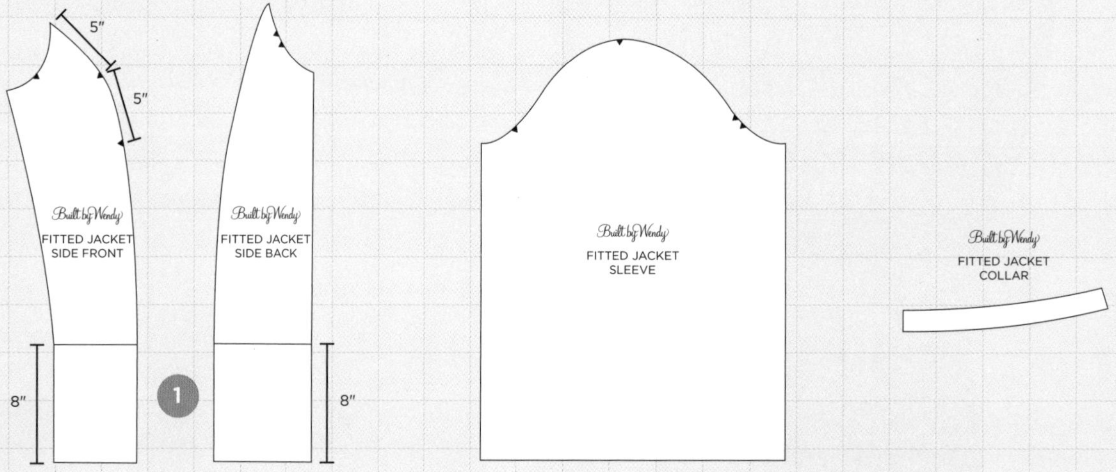

5"

5"

FITTED JACKET SIDE FRONT
Built by Wendy

FITTED JACKET SIDE BACK
Built by Wendy

FITTED JACKET SLEEVE
Built by Wendy

FITTED JACKET COLLAR
Built by Wendy

8"

1

8"

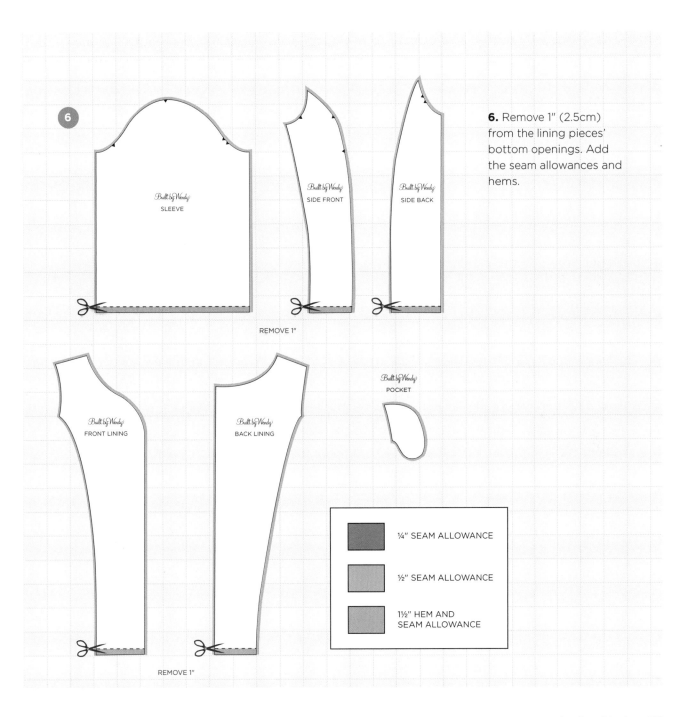

6. Remove 1" (2.5cm) from the lining pieces' bottom openings. Add the seam allowances and hems.

6

Built by Wendy
SLEEVE

Built by Wendy
SIDE FRONT

Built by Wendy
SIDE BACK

REMOVE 1"

Built by Wendy
FRONT LINING

Built by Wendy
BACK LINING

Built by Wendy
POCKET

REMOVE 1"

	¼" SEAM ALLOWANCE
	½" SEAM ALLOWANCE
	1½" HEM AND SEAM ALLOWANCE

pattern adjustments

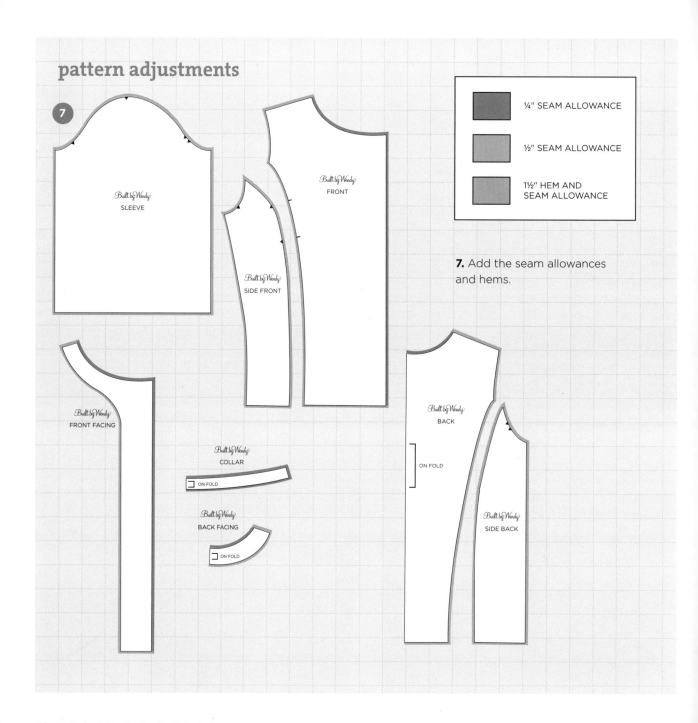

7. Add the seam allowances and hems.

■	¼" SEAM ALLOWANCE
■	½" SEAM ALLOWANCE
■	1½" HEM AND SEAM ALLOWANCE

Built by Wendy
SLEEVE

Built by Wendy
FRONT

Built by Wendy
SIDE FRONT

Built by Wendy
FRONT FACING

Built by Wendy
COLLAR
ON FOLD

Built by Wendy
BACK FACING
ON FOLD

Built by Wendy
BACK
ON FOLD

Built by Wendy
SIDE BACK

cutting

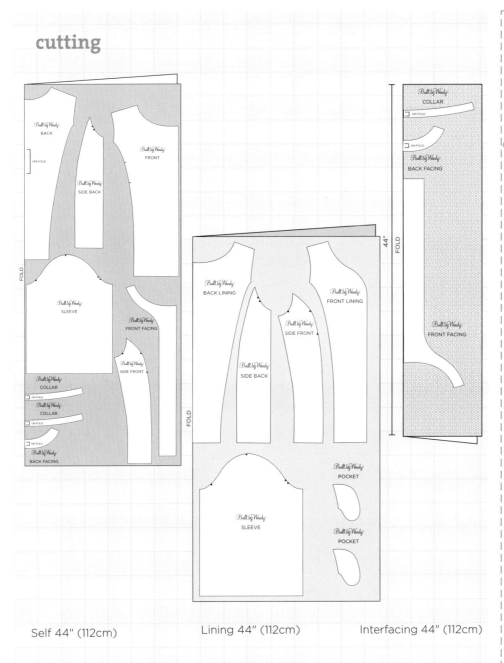

Self 44" (112cm)

Lining 44" (112cm)

Interfacing 44" (112cm)

ALTERNATIVE

Singin' in the Raincoat

This same pattern takes on a spiffy English look when made in water-repellent beige twill with a plaid lining. If you want to freshen up the classic formula, try leaving off the collar, shortening the sleeves a few inches, and slashing and spreading the sleeve so that it's gathered (and therefore, a bit girlier). Don't forget to add a hood! And try genuine horn buttons for a classy finishing touch. Who says rainy days have to be all doom and gloom?

sewing

1. With right sides together, sew the pockets to the front side pieces and the front pieces between the notches.

2. With right sides together, sew the front side pieces to the front pieces, sewing around the pockets. Do the same for the back seams (but without pockets of course!). Do the same for the lining.

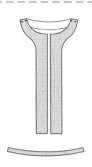

3. Attach interfacing to the collar and facings. With right sides together, sew the front to the back facing at the shoulders.

4. With right sides together, sew the front to the back at the shoulders. Do the same for the lining.

5. With right sides together, sew the sleeves to the armholes. Do the same for the lining.

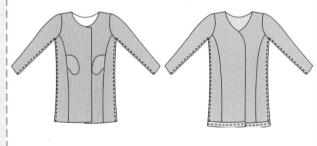

6. With right sides together, sew the front to the back at the side seams from the bottom opening up to the sleeve opening. Do the same for the lining. Hem the lining's bottom opening.

7. With right sides together, sew the collar pieces together around the sides and the top edge. Turn the collar right side out and top-stitch around the seams.

8. With right sides together, sew the collar to the neckline matching up the center back points of the collar and back pieces.

9. With right sides together, sew the lining to the facing around the ·neckline and fronts.

10. With right sides together, sew the gar-ment to the facing around neckline and fronts. Sew the front facing bottom the width of the hem.

11. Turn the garment right side out, then fold up the hem of the bottom opening and hand-stitch the lining's bottom opening to the garment hem.

12. Fold back the sleeve opening and sleeve lining opening hems and hand-stitch them together.

13. Measure the button placement carefully and sew the buttons and buttonholes where indicated, starting 2″ (5cm) down from the top edge and then spacing two more horizontal rows 4″ (10cm) apart. The vertical rows of buttons should be placed 4″ (10cm) apart.

CHAPTER 5

THE BASIC JACKET

THE QUESTION IS NOT WHETHER YOU NEED A STRAIGHT-FITTING, CASUAL JACKET— it's how many you need! The classic hip-length, not-too-snug jacket pattern we'll work with in this chapter is one of the mainstays of each Built by Wendy collection. It has traditional set-in sleeves, a great template for all sorts of casual sportswear looks. Substituting a dressy fabric on a casual style can be an interesting design technique. I've got plenty of suggestions for alternative fabrics and trims to transform the look of each project, but I also encourage you to switch things up your way!

Unlike the pattern in chapter 4, the basic jacket has no darts or body-shaping seams on the pattern. This means there are likely to be fewer sewing steps (there are no side front parts), and it also gives you a flat surface, making it the ultimate canvas for playing around with pockets (and trust me, in this chapter, wc will.) The straight body is also endlessly adaptable: You can taper or widen the silhouette for totally different look, like a poncho. Read on for more ideas on how to make the basic jacket anything but.

the jackie jacket

The boxy silhouette and elegant boatneck of this warm-weather jacket create instant polish; you'll feel like modern-day Jacqueline Onassis. The sunshine-bright linen, contrast binding, and covered buttons give it a vintage feeling, but I love the idea of tossing it over some beat-up jeans and a white tee and adding a jumble of chains and costume jewelry to modernize the look.

supplies

2 yards (1.8m) yellow linen

½ yard (46cm) white fusible interfacing

3 yards (2.7m) ½"- (13mm-) wide white bias binding

8 white 40 ligne covered buttons

TRY THESE TOO!

Chic: Silver Lurex–flecked canvas with black silk binding

Girly: Pink floral printed cotton piqué

Fall: Navy wool tweed

pattern adjustments

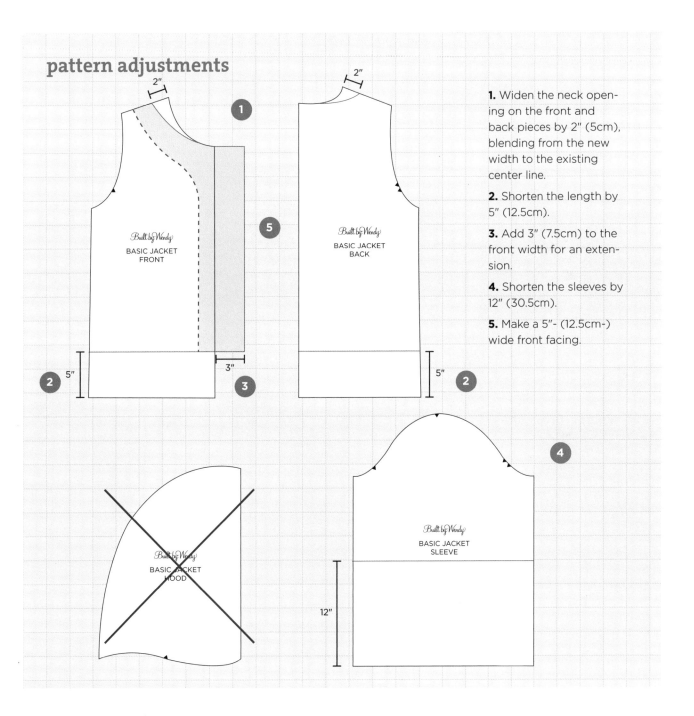

1. Widen the neck opening on the front and back pieces by 2" (5cm), blending from the new width to the existing center line.

2. Shorten the length by 5" (12.5cm).

3. Add 3" (7.5cm) to the front width for an extension.

4. Shorten the sleeves by 12" (30.5cm).

5. Make a 5"- (12.5cm-) wide front facing.

Built by Wendy
BASIC JACKET
FRONT

Built by Wendy
BASIC JACKET
BACK

Built by Wendy
BASIC JACKET
HOOD

Built by Wendy
BASIC JACKET
SLEEVE

pattern adjustments

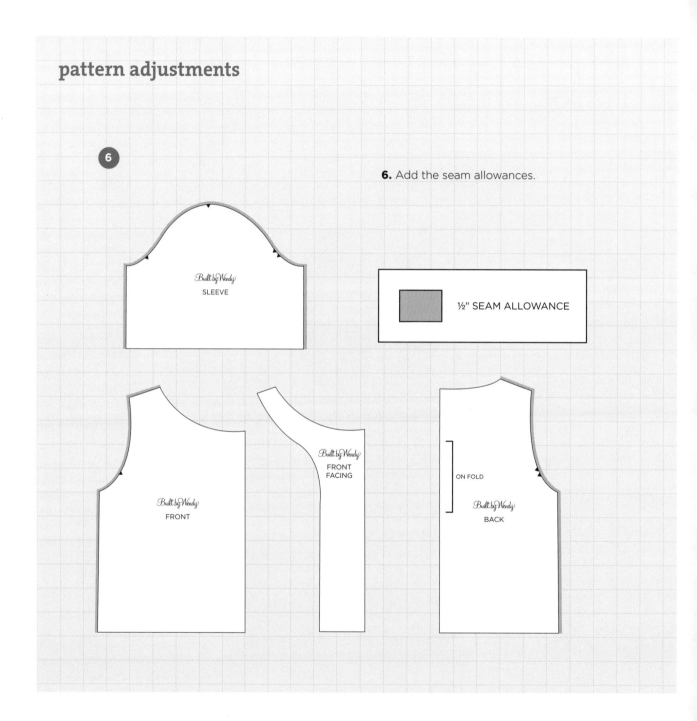

6

6. Add the seam allowances.

SLEEVE

½" SEAM ALLOWANCE

FRONT

FRONT FACING

ON FOLD

BACK

cutting

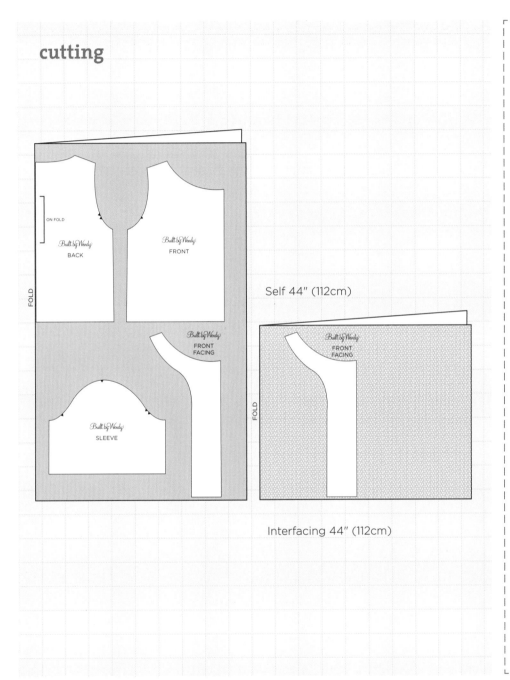

ON FOLD

FOLD

Built by Wendy
BACK

Built by Wendy
FRONT

Self 44" (112cm)

Built by Wendy
FRONT
FACING

Built by Wendy
SLEEVE

FOLD

Built by Wendy
FRONT
FACING

Interfacing 44" (112cm)

She's in the Band

The marching-band jacket is a perennial favorite among the high-fashion crowd, and it's easy to see why: It's a classic, but it's structured and makes a statement. This version is made in bright red wool with black-binding buttoned-on tabs, big gold buttons, and collar. Sew on buttons and instead of making buttonholes just take four pieces of ribbon or sewn-closed bias binding and make a buttonhole at each end. Button on to each button. Stylish and functional!

sewing

1. Attach interfacing to the front facing. With wrong sides together, pin the facing to the front.

2. With right sides together, sew the front to the back at the shoulders.

3. With right sides together, sew the sleeves to the armholes.

4. Sew the binding around the front edge and sleeve openings. Take another piece of binding and sew it around the neck ¾" (2cm) beyond the front. Then fold back the extended piece ¼" (6mm) then again ½" (13mm) so that you have a clean-finished edge. Hand-stitch on the inside of the garment.

5. With right sides together, sew the front to the back at the side seams from the bottom opening to the sleeve opening.

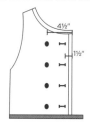

6. Sew the binding around the bottom opening, extending it ¾" (2cm) beyond the front, then fold back the extended piece ¼" (6mm), then again ½" (13mm), so you have a clean-finished edge. Hand-stitch on the inside of the garment.

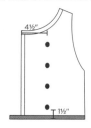

7. Attach the buttons and make the buttonholes.

PROJECT 2

code orange

Made in can't-miss safety-orange quilted nylon—a fabric usually used for visibility in hunting gear!—this fun piece not only adds warmth to hikes in the woods, but also makes a zingy city layering piece that looks utilitarian chic when combined with leggings, a big gray boyfriend sweater, and a killer pair of ankle boots. You're guaranteed to get noticed from a mile away.

supplies

1 yard (91cm) neon orange quilted nylon
3 yards (2.7m) brown bias binding
24" (61cm) silver separating zipper

TRY THESE TOO!
Chic: Gray quilted flannel
Sporty: Navy cotton fleece
Preppy: White cotton piqué

pattern adjustments

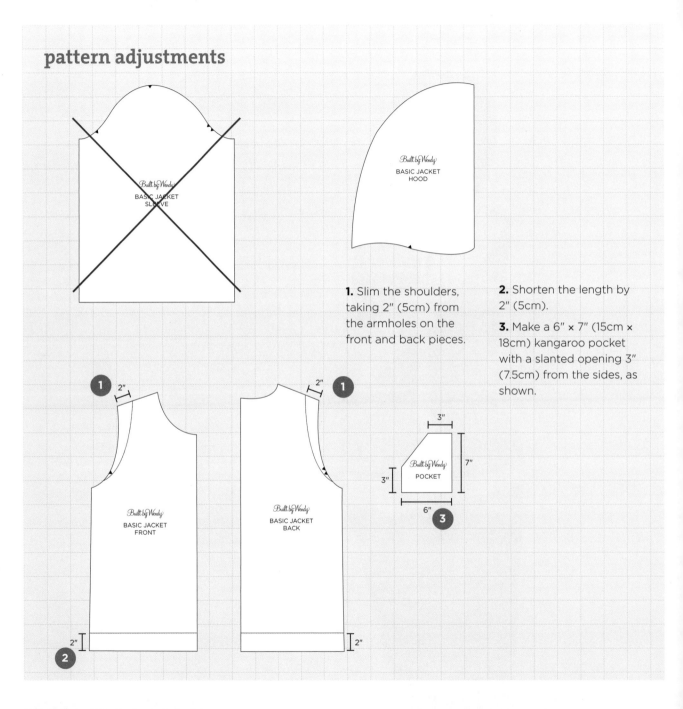

1. Slim the shoulders, taking 2″ (5cm) from the armholes on the front and back pieces.

2. Shorten the length by 2″ (5cm).

3. Make a 6″ × 7″ (15cm × 18cm) kangaroo pocket with a slanted opening 3″ (7.5cm) from the sides, as shown.

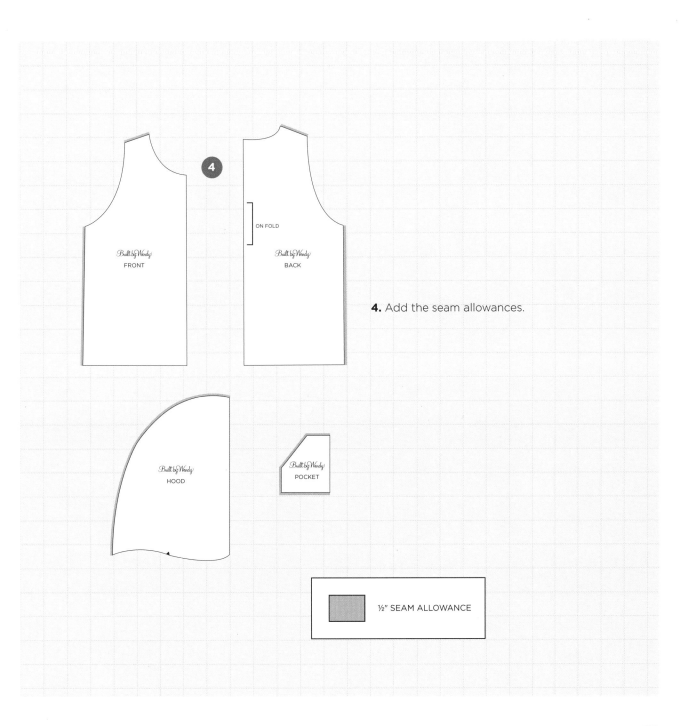

4. Add the seam allowances.

1/2" SEAM ALLOWANCE

cutting

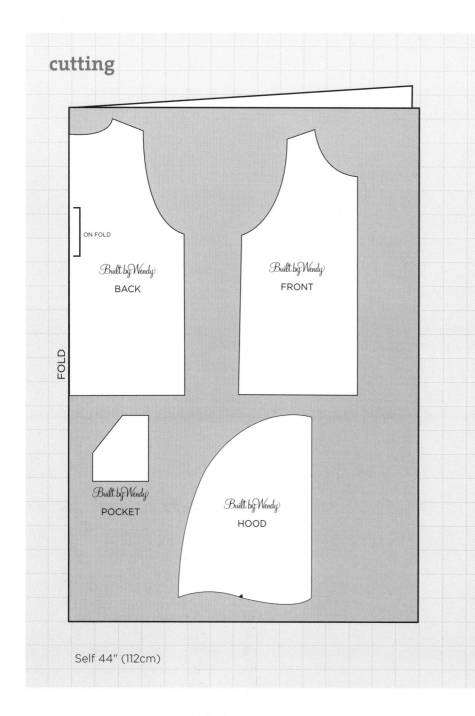

ON FOLD

FOLD

Built by Wendy
BACK

Built by Wendy
FRONT

Built by Wendy
POCKET

Built by Wendy
HOOD

Self 44" (112cm)

Gone Fishing

A fisherman-inspired look in khaki ripstop is another variation on this shape that works equally well on nature walks and city sidewalks. Remove the hood and add tons of pockets in various sizes—have fun with them! Try picking up some D-rings and cotton twill tape to make loops to adjust the fit. Cute vintage outdoorsman patches (why not rifle through your Uncle Gary's garage?) will give it an authentically rugged feeling.

sewing

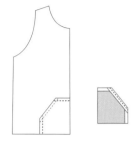

1. Hem the opening and the inside edges of the pocket pieces. Topstitch the hemmed edges of the pockets to the front pieces, aligning raw edges with opening and bottom edges of front.

2. With right sides together, sew the front to the back at the shoulders.

3. With right sides together, sew the hood pieces together along the curved edge.

4. With right sides together, sew the hood to the neckline.

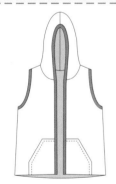

5. Sew the binding around the front opening, hood, and armholes.

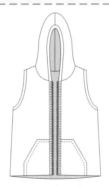

6. Separate the zipper and attach each side behind the binding at the front opening. Note: This is a different method than sewing in a zipper using the seam allowances.

7. With right sides together, sew the front to the back at the side seams.

8. Sew the binding around the bottom opening.

the chic poncho

Every year, as soon as the leaves start to turn, I start to daydream about traipsing through the woods in a cozy poncho. Forget about the boho-Pocahontas look—with the right silhouette, ponchos can look so chic. This crisp, apple-red, boiled-wool version is the perfect layer to toss on over a chunky Irish-style knit sweater to keep warm in winter. Plus, it's the easiest project ever!

supplies

3 yards (2.7m) red boiled wool
10 yards (9.1m) black wool binding
6 size 40 ligne gold buttons

TRY THESE TOO!
Rustic: Brown-and-navy striped wool
Summer: Eggplant linen
*Sporty: Navy wool felt with white-and-
    yellow striped trim*

pattern adjustments

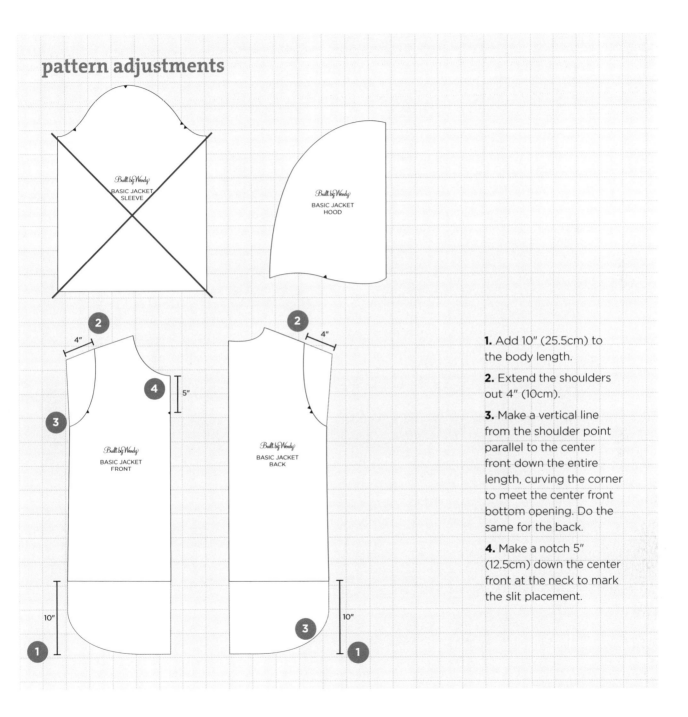

1. Add 10″ (25.5cm) to the body length.

2. Extend the shoulders out 4″ (10cm).

3. Make a vertical line from the shoulder point parallel to the center front down the entire length, curving the corner to meet the center front bottom opening. Do the same for the back.

4. Make a notch 5″ (12.5cm) down the center front at the neck to mark the slit placement.

pattern adjustments

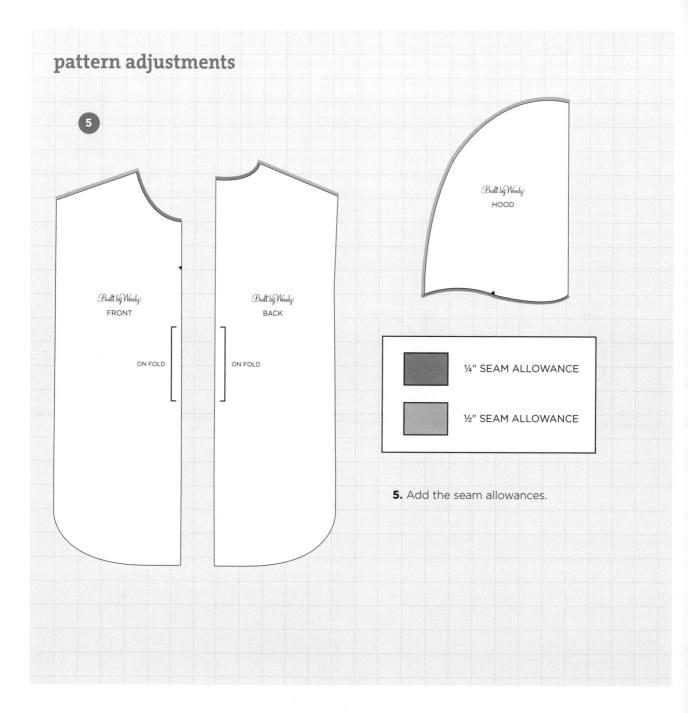

5

Built by Wendy
FRONT

ON FOLD

Built by Wendy
BACK

ON FOLD

Built by Wendy
HOOD

¼" SEAM ALLOWANCE

½" SEAM ALLOWANCE

5. Add the seam allowances.

cutting

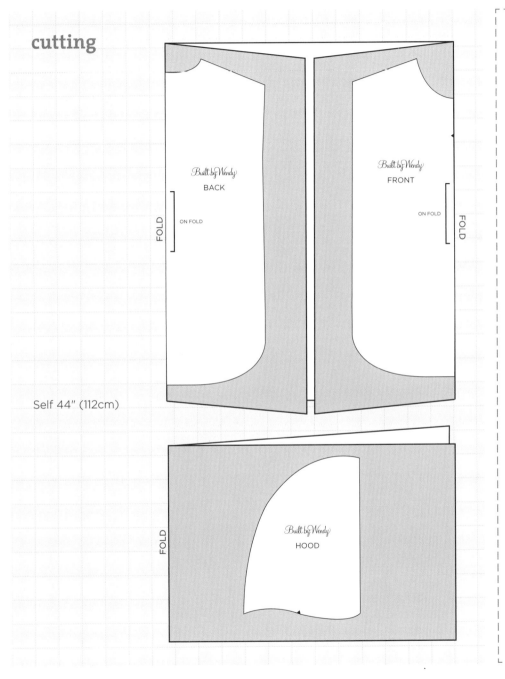

Built by Wendy
BACK

FOLD

ON FOLD

Built by Wendy
FRONT

ON FOLD

FOLD

Self 44" (112cm)

FOLD

Built by Wendy
HOOD

ALTERNATIVE

Toss-Over Trench

You can make this same shape in water-repellent khaki twill for a pullover trench that's a little bit Burberry, a little bit Casablanca. A waist-cinching belt (add a buckle) makes for a dra-matically chic, ladylike silhouette that keeps you dry, too. Use the collar from chapter 6, and add front and back yokes. It's so fun and glamorous to wear, you may start wishing for rain!

sewing

1. With right sides together, sew the front to the back at the shoulders.

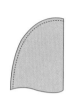

2. With right sides together, sew the hood pieces together along the curved edge.

3. With right sides together, sew the hood to the neckline.

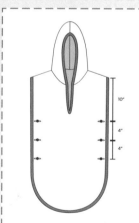

4. Sew binding around neckline, hood, and outer edge.

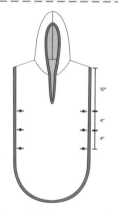

5. Sew the buttons and buttonholes 1½″ (3.8cm) in from the edge.

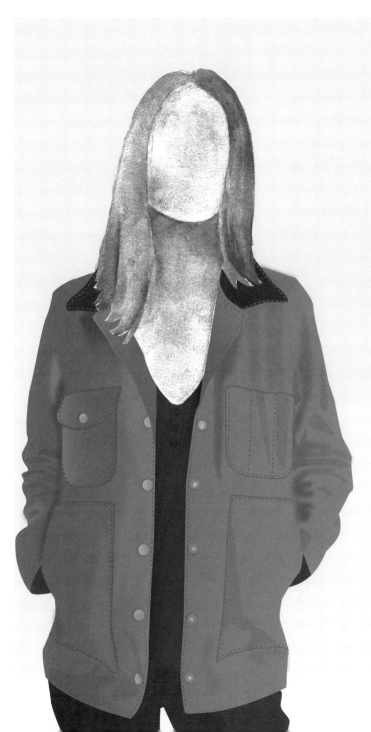

the carpenter jacket

Sometimes, like when you're working in your art studio or kicking around on a casual weekend, a simple jacket is all you want. Of course, really good simple jackets are hard to find, which is why you'll love my update on the work-wear staple. In straight-cut canvas with a corduroy collar and pencil pocket, it takes its cues from your boyfriend's old fave, but it's designed to hang just right—slouchy but still flattering—on you!

supplies

2 yards (1.8m) beige cotton canvas
½ yard (46cm) brown cotton corduroy
1 yard (91cm) black fusible interfacing
6 size 24 brass snaps
Snap fastener

TRY THESE TOO!
Chic: Black wool felt with a shearling collar
Tough: Brown leatherette
Preppy: Khaki cotton twill

pattern adjustments

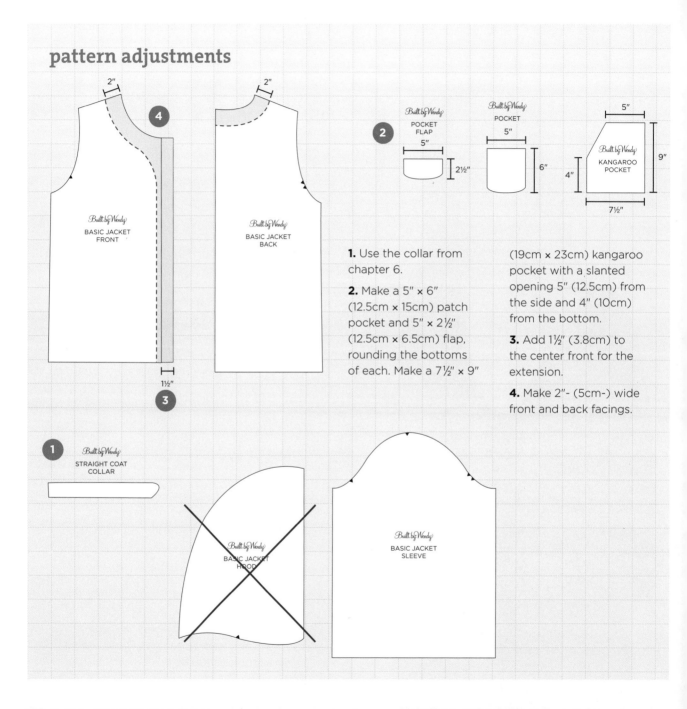

2"

2"

Built by Wendy
BASIC JACKET
FRONT

Built by Wendy
BASIC JACKET
BACK

4

Built by Wendy
POCKET
FLAP

5"

2½"

Built by Wendy
POCKET

5"

6"

2

5"

Built by Wendy
KANGAROO
POCKET

9"

4"

7½"

1½"

3

1

Built by Wendy
STRAIGHT COAT
COLLAR

Built by Wendy
BASIC JACKET
HOOD

Built by Wendy
BASIC JACKET
SLEEVE

1. Use the collar from chapter 6.

2. Make a 5″ × 6″ (12.5cm × 15cm) patch pocket and 5″ × 2½″ (12.5cm × 6.5cm) flap, rounding the bottoms of each. Make a 7½″ × 9″ (19cm × 23cm) kangaroo pocket with a slanted opening 5″ (12.5cm) from the side and 4″ (10cm) from the bottom.

3. Add 1½″ (3.8cm) to the center front for the extension.

4. Make 2″- (5cm-) wide front and back facings.

pattern adjustments

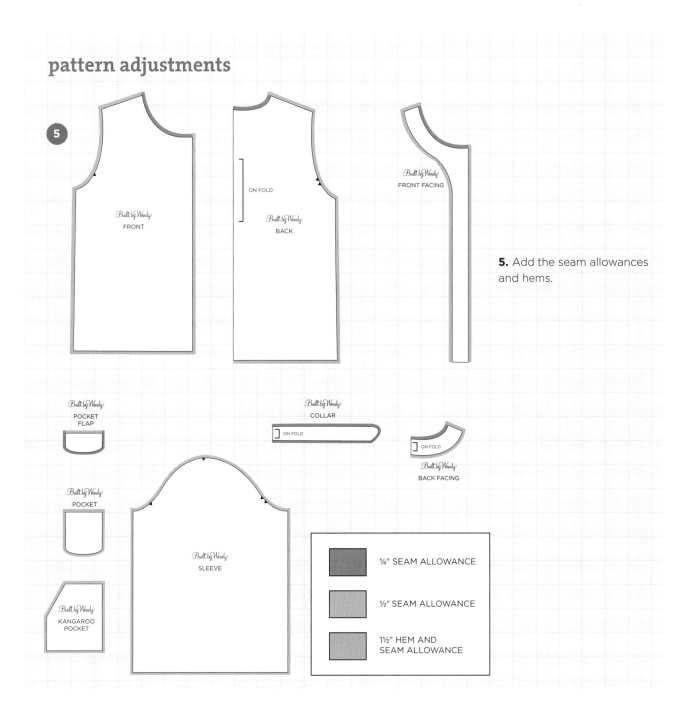

5. Add the seam allowances and hems.

5

ON FOLD

Built by Wendy
FRONT

Built by Wendy
BACK

Built by Wendy
FRONT FACING

Built by Wendy
POCKET
FLAP

Built by Wendy
COLLAR

ON FOLD

ON FOLD

Built by Wendy
BACK FACING

Built by Wendy
POCKET

Built by Wendy
SLEEVE

Built by Wendy
KANGAROO
POCKET

¼" SEAM ALLOWANCE

½" SEAM ALLOWANCE

1½" HEM AND
SEAM ALLOWANCE

cutting

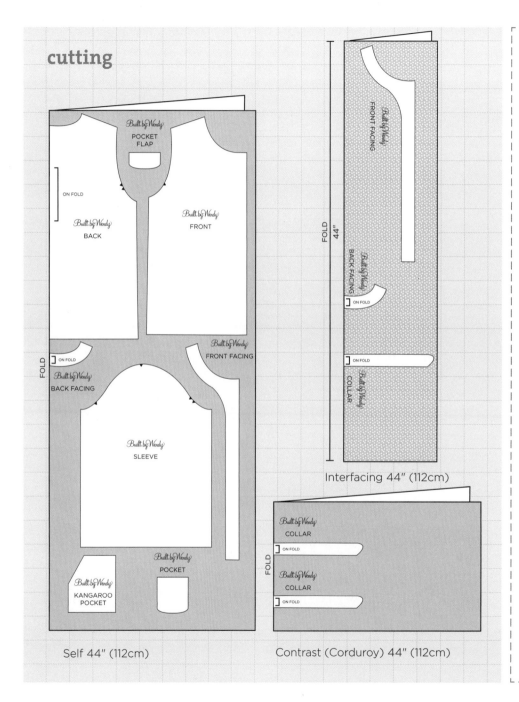

ON FOLD

Built by Wendy
POCKET
FLAP

Built by Wendy
BACK

Built by Wendy
FRONT

FOLD

ON FOLD

Built by Wendy
BACK FACING

Built by Wendy
FRONT FACING

Built by Wendy
SLEEVE

Built by Wendy
KANGAROO
POCKET

Built by Wendy
POCKET

Self 44" (112cm)

FOLD
44"

Built by Wendy
FRONT FACING

Built by Wendy
BACK FACING

ON FOLD

ON FOLD

Built by Wendy
COLLAR

Interfacing 44" (112cm)

FOLD

Built by Wendy
COLLAR

ON FOLD

Built by Wendy
COLLAR

ON FOLD

Contrast (Corduroy) 44" (112cm)

ALTERNATIVE

Double Vision

This style looks complicated, but is actually quite simple. Just make a short sleeve and a full-length sleeve, and sew them on at the same time. Instead of a contrast collar, use the stand-up collar from chapter 4. Factor in a luxurious wool weave, and this seemingly basic jacket really offers that something extra. After all, true style is in the details!

sewing

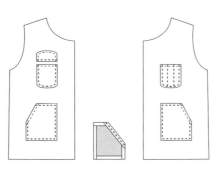

1. Hem the pockets and sew the flap pieces right sides together, turn them right side out, and top-stitch around the seamed edges. Then, topstitch them to the front pieces. For placement I would hold up the front piece to your chest in the mirror and pin pockets in the position you prefer. For the pencil pocket, you can sew it as you would do a normal patch pocket, but then topstitch two rows of stitching as shown, dividing the width of the pocket in thirds to make equal placement of rows.

2. With right sides together, sew the front to the back at the shoulders.

3. With right sides together, sew the sleeves to the armholes.

4. With right sides together, sew the front to the back at the side seams from the bottom opening up to the sleeve opening.

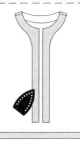

5. Attach the interfacing to the facings and the collar. Then with right sides together, sew the front facing to the back facing at the shoulders.

sewing

6. With right sides together, sew the collar pieces together around the sides and top edge. Turn the collar right side out and topstitch.

7. With right sides together, sew the collar to the neckline, leaving ½" (13mm) between the collar and the extension edge.

8. With right sides together, sew the facing to the neckline, front, and bottom opening, sandwiching the collar. Understitch the facing.

9. Hem the sleeve and bottom openings. Topstitch the front as shown.

10. Attach the snaps to the front and the pocket flap, beginning with the top snap 1" (2.5cm) down from the neck and the second snap 2" (5cm) up from the bottom opening, then place snaps equally between those two points.

the updated jean jacket

Not all jean jackets are created equal. This vintage-inspired version has a slight seventies feeling, with a heavy brass zipper in front instead of the usual snaps. The pockets shown here give it a utilitarian look, but feel free to have fun playing around with the shapes! Use contrast denim thread for a classic work-wear vibe, or matching thread for a sleeker, office-friendly update.

supplies

2 yards (1.8m) indigo denim
24" (61cm) separating brass zipper
4 size 24 brass snaps (and fastener)

TRY THESE TOO!
Summer: Hot pink lightweight cotton
Fall: Brown wool tweed
Chic: Navy Ultrasuede

pattern adjustments

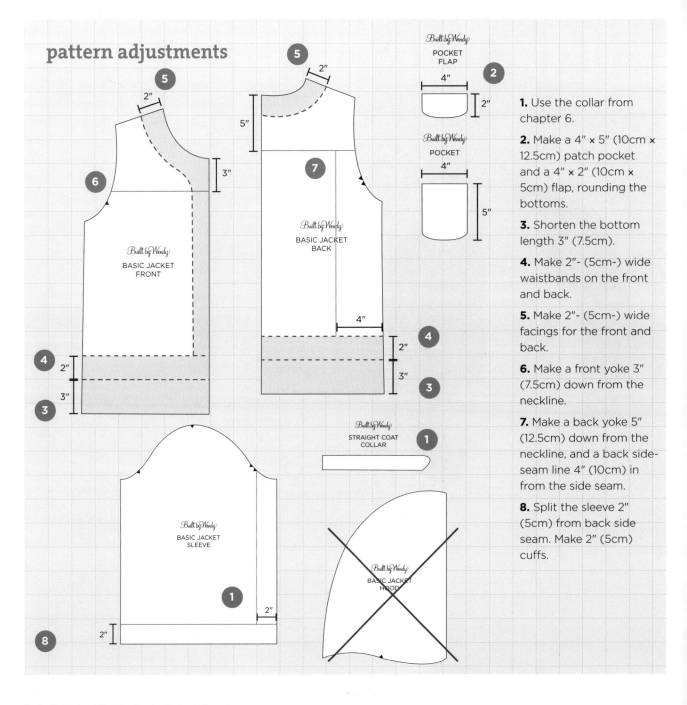

1. Use the collar from chapter 6.

2. Make a 4" × 5" (10cm × 12.5cm) patch pocket and a 4" × 2" (10cm × 5cm) flap, rounding the bottoms.

3. Shorten the bottom length 3" (7.5cm).

4. Make 2"- (5cm-) wide waistbands on the front and back.

5. Make 2"- (5cm-) wide facings for the front and back.

6. Make a front yoke 3" (7.5cm) down from the neckline.

7. Make a back yoke 5" (12.5cm) down from the neckline, and a back side-seam line 4" (10cm) in from the side seam.

8. Split the sleeve 2" (5cm) from back side seam. Make 2" (5cm) cuffs.

pattern adjustments

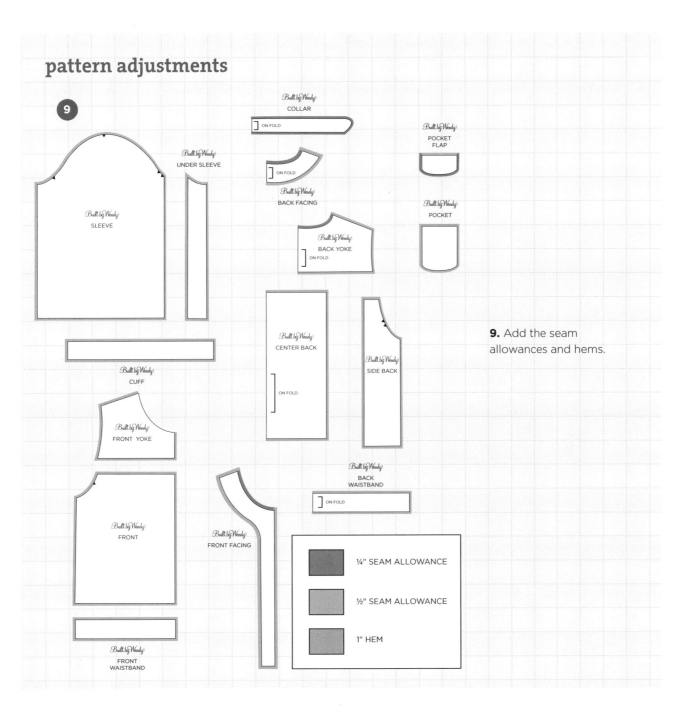

9. Add the seam allowances and hems.

cutting

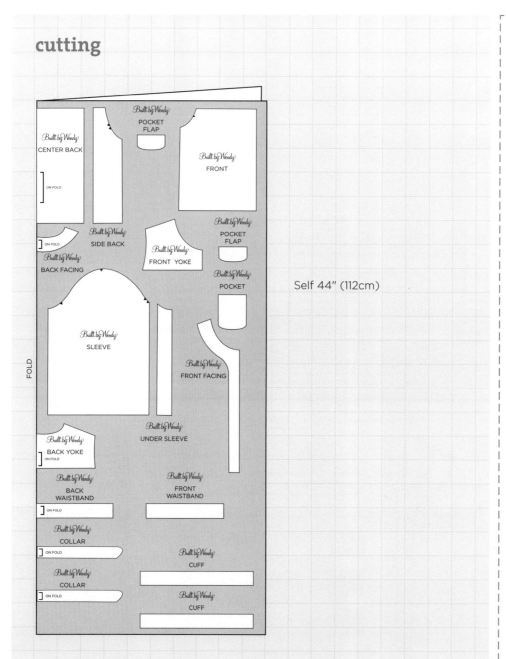

Self 44" (112cm)

ALTERNATIVE

Fly Girl

Why not channel your inner Amelia Earhart and make this jacket in leatherette with a faux-fur collar? Just make the collar slightly taller, round the tips, and change the shape, size, and placement of the patch pockets as shown. I recommend lining the body to give it a more solid cool-weather quality. Toss on some high-waisted jeans and a pair of aviator glasses, and there'll be no mistaking who's *Top Gun*!

sewing

1. With right sides together, sew the front facings to the back facing at the shoulders.

2. With right sides together, sew the pocket flap pieces together. Turn right side out and topstitch.

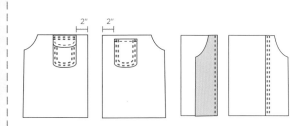

3. Hem the pockets and topstitch the pockets and flaps to the front pieces. Place pockets and flap 2″ (5cm) from the center front raw edge so that pocket flap top raw edge is flush with the yoke raw edge.

4. With right sides together, sew side back to center back. Press open and double topstitch the seam.

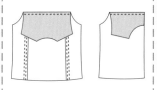

5. With right sides together, sew the back yoke to the back and the front yoke to the front, sandwiching the pocket flaps. Double topstitch the seams.

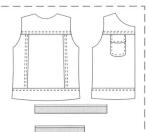

6. Fold back the top edges of the waistbands, then with wrong side to right side, topstitch to the body so that bottom openings edges are matched up.

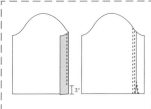

7. With right sides together, sew the side sleeve to the sleeve, leaving 3″ (7.5cm) open at the bottom opening. Double topstitch the seam to one side until you get to the opening, and then press open flat and topstitch on each side of opening.

8. With right sides together, sew the front to the back at the shoulders.

sewing

9. With right sides together, sew the sleeve to the armhole.

10. With right sides together, sew the front to the back at the side seams from the bottom opening to the sleeve opening.

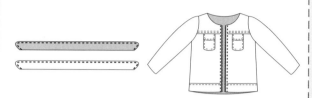

11. With right sides together, sew the collar pieces together around the outer edge. Turn them right side out, and topstitch around the outer edge.

12. Attach the zipper so that the teeth begin $3/4''$ (2cm) below the neckline.

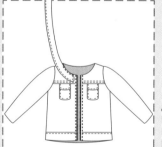

13. With right sides together, sew the collar to the neckline.

14. With right sides together, sew the facings around the neckline, sandwiching the collar.

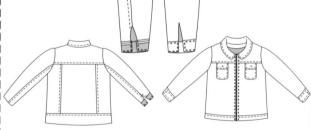

15. With right sides together, sew the cuff to the sleeve opening. Then fold the cuff-facing inner edge, sew the cuff facing to the cuff around the outer edge and sides, turn right side out and topstitch around entire cuff.

16. Flip the facing to the inside of the garment, fold back the seam allowance of the facing's front edge, and topstitch the front facing to the zipper tape. Attach snaps to the cuffs, pockets, and pocket flaps.

PROJECT 6

g.i. jane

I can't get enough of classic olive-green
military anoraks. They're chic but never
feel like they're trying too hard; they add
a touch of toughness to dressy outfits but
are great for just bumming around, too. This
wool tweed version is based on a best-
selling Built by Wendy pattern, and it fits
the female form nicely. It's roomy enough
to wear with chunky sweaters, but unlike
surplus-store versions, it'll never make you
look sloppy.

supplies

2 yards (1.8m) olive green wool tweed

3 yards (2.7m) olive green cotton cording

1 yard (91cm) of 1"- (2.5cm-) wide olive green
ribbon

1 yard (91cm) black fusible interfacing

9 olive green 34 ligne buttons

TRY THESE TOO!
Rainy Day: Khaki water-repellent twill
Spring: Beige linen
Chic: Brown cashmere

pattern adjustments

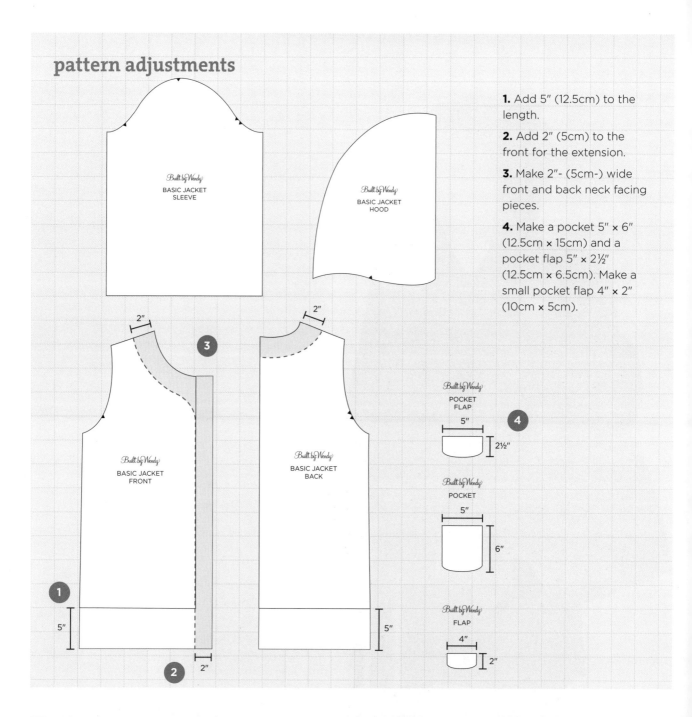

1. Add 5" (12.5cm) to the length.

2. Add 2" (5cm) to the front for the extension.

3. Make 2"- (5cm-) wide front and back neck facing pieces.

4. Make a pocket 5" × 6" (12.5cm × 15cm) and a pocket flap 5" × 2½" (12.5cm × 6.5cm). Make a small pocket flap 4" × 2" (10cm × 5cm).

Built by Wendy
BASIC JACKET
SLEEVE

Built by Wendy
BASIC JACKET
HOOD

Built by Wendy
BASIC JACKET
FRONT

Built by Wendy
BASIC JACKET
BACK

Built by Wendy
POCKET
FLAP
5"
2½"

Built by Wendy
POCKET
5"
6"

Built by Wendy
FLAP
4"
2"

2"

2"

5"

5"

2"

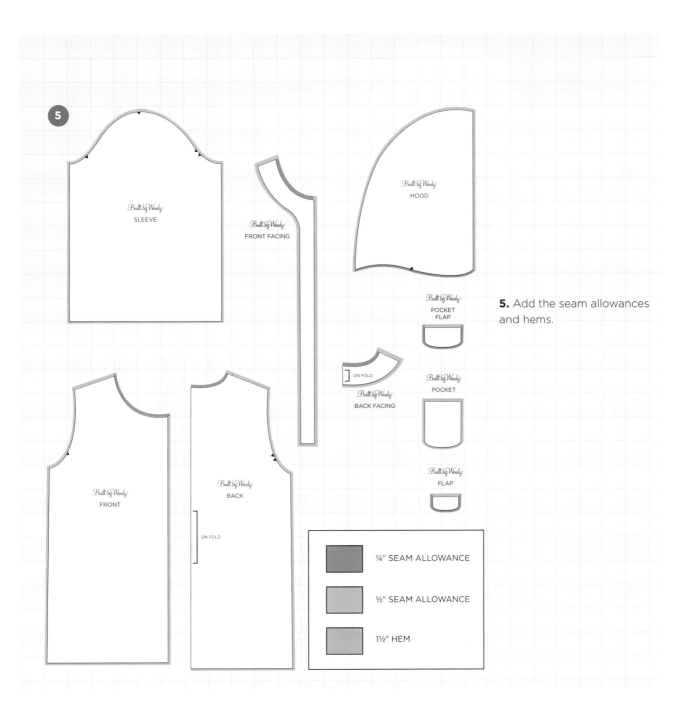

5. Add the seam allowances and hems.

SLEEVE

FRONT FACING

HOOD

POCKET FLAP

POCKET

BACK FACING

ON FOLD

FLAP

FRONT

BACK

ON FOLD

¼" SEAM ALLOWANCE

½" SEAM ALLOWANCE

1½" HEM

cutting

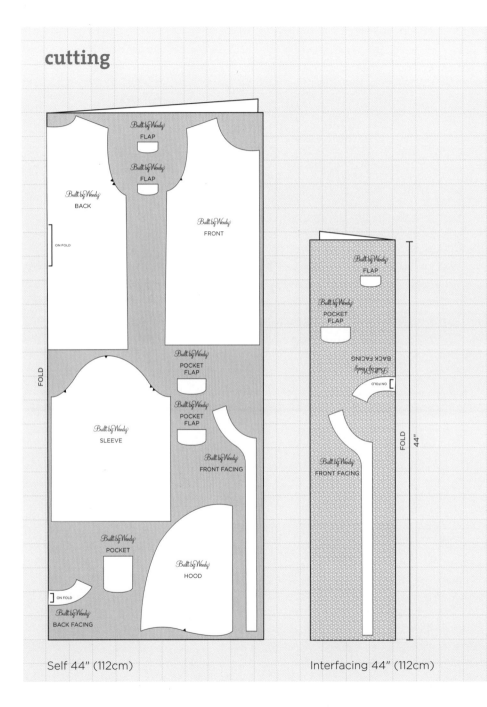

Self 44" (112cm)

Interfacing 44" (112cm)

Labels within the cutting layout:
- Built by Wendy FLAP
- Built by Wendy FLAP
- Built by Wendy BACK
- ON FOLD
- Built by Wendy FRONT
- FOLD
- Built by Wendy POCKET FLAP
- Built by Wendy SLEEVE
- Built by Wendy POCKET FLAP
- Built by Wendy FRONT FACING
- Built by Wendy POCKET
- Built by Wendy HOOD
- ON FOLD
- Built by Wendy BACK FACING
- Built by Wendy FLAP
- Built by Wendy POCKET FLAP
- Built by Wendy BACK FACING
- ON FOLD
- Built by Wendy FRONT FACING
- FOLD
- 44"

ALTERNATIVE

New Navy

This navy cotton twill jacket uses the same pattern as the wool anorak, but you'd never know because it drapes so differently. Just use the collar from chapter 6, and topstitch white ribbon stripes on the biceps of each sleeve, and there you have it: a nautical treasure, perfect for tossing on over tank dresses or shorts and keeping breezes at bay all spring and summer long.

sewing

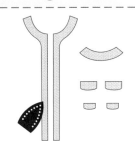

1. Attach the interfacing to the facings and the pocket flaps.

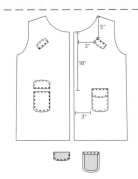

2. Hem the pockets. With right sides together, sew the flap pieces together and turn right side out. Topstitch the pockets and the pocket flaps to the front pieces.

3. With right sides together, sew the front to the back at the shoulders. Do the same for the facings.

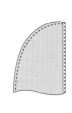

4. With right sides together, sew the hood pieces together. Hem the opening.

5. With right sides together, sew the hood to the neckline.

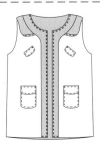

6. With right sides together, sew the facing to the neckline, front, and bottom opening, sandwiching the hood inside. Turn the facing to the inside and understitch the seam allowance.

7. With right sides together, sew the sleeves to the armholes.

8. With right sides together, sew the front to the back along the side seams from the bottom opening to up the sleeve opening.

sewing

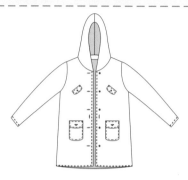

9. Hem the sleeve and bottom openings. Top-stitch the front piece as shown.

10. Attach buttons and make buttonholes for front and pockets. Begin place-ment 1″ (2.5cm) down from the neck, then space evenly to 5″ (12.5cm) above the bottom open-ing. Attach buttons onto pocket flaps, sewing through the flap and body. Make two buttonholes 1″ (2.5cm) long placed 3″ (7.5cm) in from the front edge for the waist tunnel opening. To find the place-ment of the waist, try on the jacket and mark where you prefer it to be.

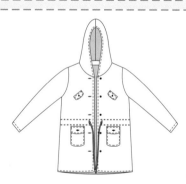

11. Topstitch the ribbon inside the body around the waist, covering the waist buttonholes.

12. Insert the cording into the tunnel and knot the ends.

the column coat

Attention minimalists: Meet your new favorite coat! This knee-length, straight zip-front coat in gray wool felt with a face-framing stand-up collar has a sophisticated silhouette that will make an impression at work, dinner parties, and gallery openings. If the urban Zen look isn't your thing, you can make it anything but basic with embroidery, appliqués, or other fun trim, or use the simple shape to spotlight a bold color, like chartreuse.

supplies

2 yards (1.8m) gray wool felt
2 yards (1.8m) gray lining
36" (91cm) silver separating zipper

TRY THESE TOO!
Sporty: Blue nylon ripstop
Spring: Light blue cotton twill
Chic: Burgundy cashmere

pattern adjustments

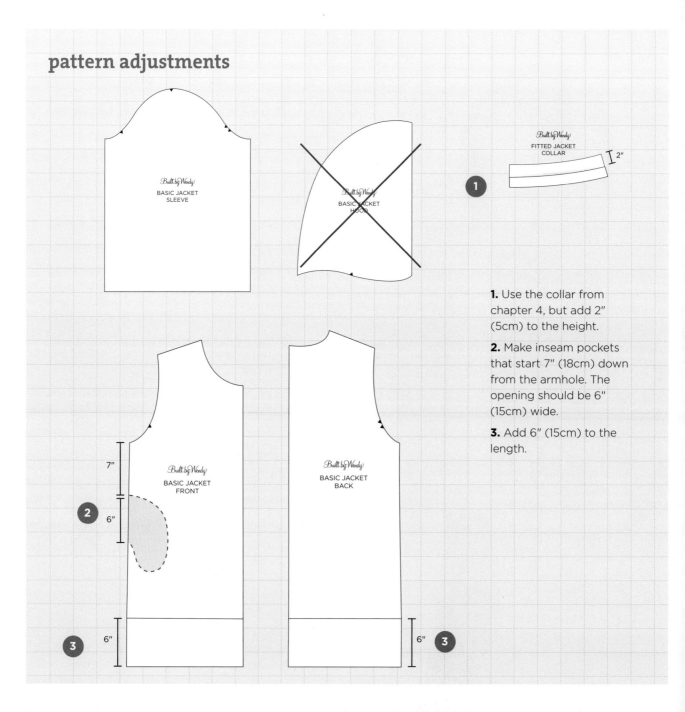

Built by Wendy
BASIC JACKET
SLEEVE

Built by Wendy
BASIC JACKET
HOOD

Built by Wendy
FITTED JACKET
COLLAR

2"

1

7"

2

6"

Built by Wendy
BASIC JACKET
FRONT

Built by Wendy
BASIC JACKET
BACK

3   6"

6"   **3**

1. Use the collar from chapter 4, but add 2" (5cm) to the height.

2. Make inseam pockets that start 7" (18cm) down from the armhole. The opening should be 6" (15cm) wide.

3. Add 6" (15cm) to the length.

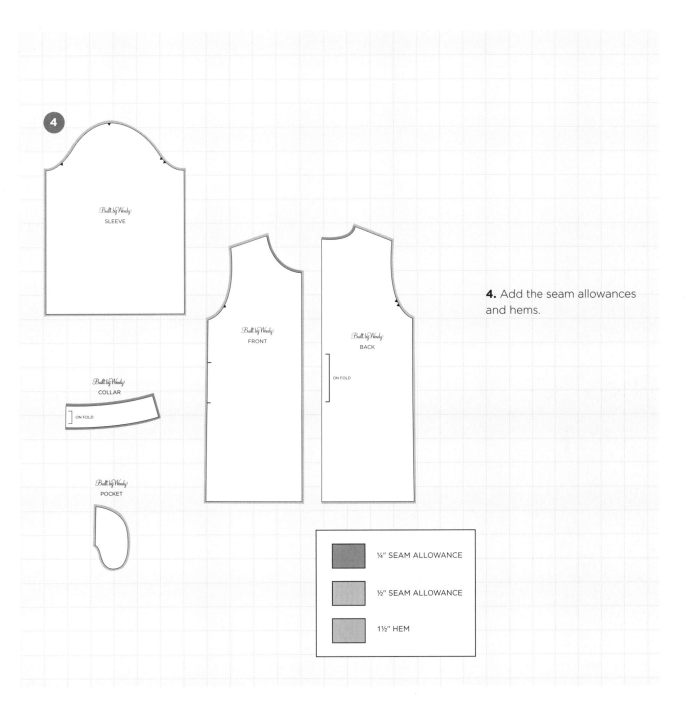

4. Add the seam allowances and hems.

Built by Wendy
SLEEVE

Built by Wendy
FRONT

Built by Wendy
BACK

ON FOLD

Built by Wendy
COLLAR

ON FOLD

Built by Wendy
POCKET

	¼" SEAM ALLOWANCE
	½" SEAM ALLOWANCE
	1½" HEM

cutting

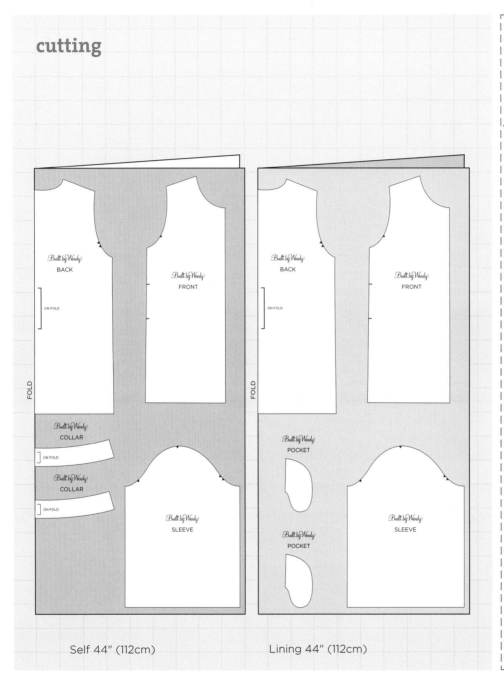

Self 44" (112cm)

Lining 44" (112cm)

Labels within diagram:
- *Built by Wendy* BACK — ON FOLD — FOLD
- *Built by Wendy* FRONT — ON FOLD
- *Built by Wendy* COLLAR — ON FOLD
- *Built by Wendy* COLLAR — ON FOLD
- *Built by Wendy* SLEEVE
- *Built by Wendy* BACK — ON FOLD — FOLD
- *Built by Wendy* FRONT
- *Built by Wendy* POCKET
- *Built by Wendy* POCKET
- *Built by Wendy* SLEEVE

The Belted Bell-Sleeve Coat

I love the dramatic look of bell sleeves on a jacket or coat; it really adds impact to after-dark looks. To make this version, simply shorten the sleeve a few inches (5cm–10cm) and slash and spread it about 4" (10cm) to make a nice bell shape. Add a belt and belt loops. Made without lining in a lightweight, dreamy silk taffeta, it's the perfect cover-up for a black-tie wedding in springtime.

sewing

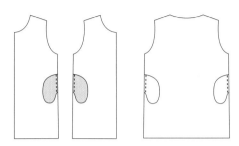

1. With right sides together, sew the pockets to the side seams of the front and back pieces.

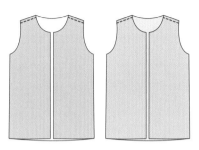

2. With right sides together, sew the front to the back at the shoulders. Do the same for the lining.

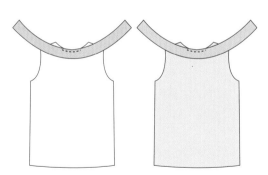

3. With right sides together, sew one collar piece to the neckline. Sew the other collar piece to the lining neckline. Always begin sewing collars at the center back points.

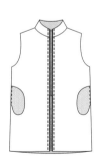

4. Attach the zipper starting zipper teeth ½″ (13mm) from the collar's top edge.

sewing

5. With right sides together, sew the sleeves to the armholes. Do the same for the lining.

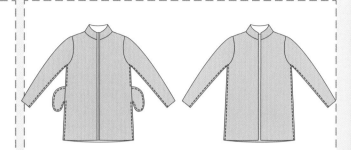

6. With right sides together, sew the front to the back at the side seams from the bottom opening, around the pockets, to the sleeve opening. Do the same for the lining (but here there are no pockets to sew around).

 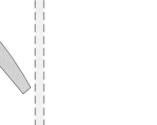

7. With right sides together, sew the lining collar to the body collar around the top edge. Understitch the seam allowance.

8. Fold back the front lining's seam allowance and hand-stitch it to the front zipper tape.

9. Hand-stitch the bottom opening hem to the lining's bottom opening hem.

10. Hand-stitch the sleeve opening hem to the sleeve opening lining.

good style hunting

This style has been a part of my collection for a couple of years now; it keeps selling out and my customers just keep asking for it to come back! I think it's been such a hit because it's ultrachic and outdoorsy at the same time. I took the inspiration from classic hunting jackets—and the black-and-grey tartan wool and amazing pocket and epaulet details reflect that—but the shape feels vaguely French in its flattering proportion.

supplies

2 yards (1.8m) black-and-grey wool buffalo plaid
2 yards (1.8m) black lining
1 yard (91cm) black fusible interfacing
11 black 36 ligne buttons

TRY THESE TOO!
Chic: Dark indigo denim
Spring: Purple-and-navy plaid linen
Holiday: Red-and-burgundy wool bouclé

pattern adjustments

BASIC JACKET
SLEEVE

Built by Wendy

BASIC JACKET
HOOD

Built by Wendy

FITTED JACKET
COLLAR

Built by Wendy

1"

1"

④

EPAULETTE

Built by Wendy

1¼"

4"

③

FRONT
EXTENSION

Built by Wendy

3"

BASIC JACKET
FRONT

Built by Wendy

BASIC JACKET
BACK

Built by Wendy

⑤

FLAP

Built by Wendy

4"

2"

POCKET
FLAP

Built by Wendy

5"

2½"

POCKET

Built by Wendy

5"

6"

1"   2"

①   ②

1. Remove 1" (2.5cm) from the front. Trace this front piece for the lining and put it aside.

2. Make a 2"- (5cm-) wide front extension piece.

3. Make a front yoke by splitting the front 3" (7.5cm) down from the neck.

4. Add 1" (2.5cm) to the height and 1" (2.5cm) to the width of the collar from chapter 4.

5. Make a 5" × 6" (12.5cm × 15cm) pocket, 5" × 2½" (12.5cm × 6.5cm) flap, 4" × 2" (10cm × 5cm) small flap, and 1¼" × 4" (3cm × 10cm) epaulettes as shown.

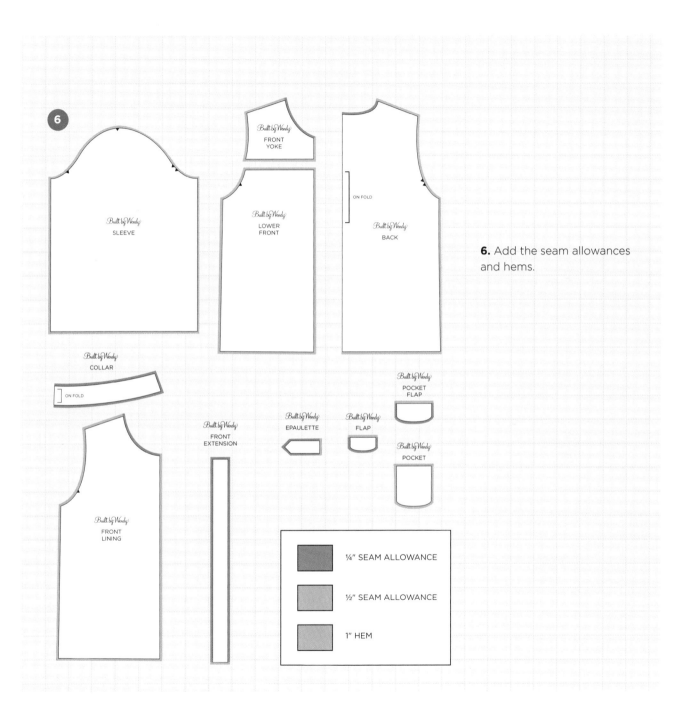

6. Add the seam allowances and hems.

¼" SEAM ALLOWANCE	
½" SEAM ALLOWANCE	
1" HEM	

SLEEVE

FRONT YOKE

LOWER FRONT

BACK

ON FOLD

COLLAR

ON FOLD

FRONT LINING

FRONT EXTENSION

EPAULETTE

FLAP

POCKET FLAP

POCKET

cutting

Self 44" (112cm)

Lining 44" (112cm)

Interfacing 44" (112cm)

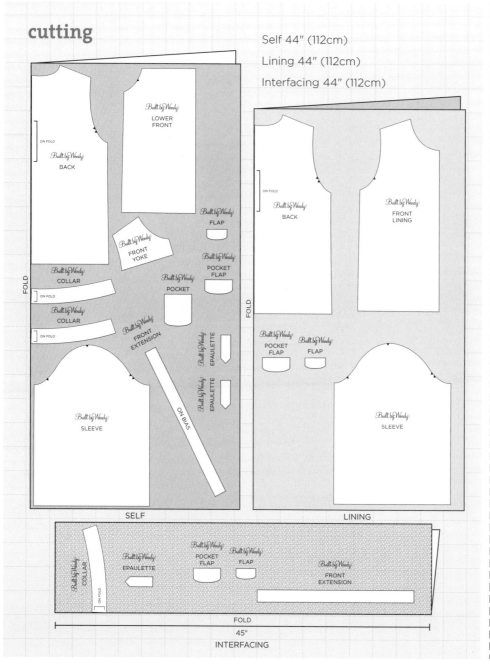

SELF

LINING

FOLD

45"

INTERFACING

The Workout Wind-breaker

In bright, color-blocked nylon, this same pattern can take on an athletic eighties vibe, although it's better suited to the dance floor than the gym. To make it, change up the pockets to make them kangaroo-style, and leave off the pocket flaps and epaulettes. Forgo the lining, too, and insert elastic into the sleeve and bottom openings. Rock it with black skinnies, eyeliner, and plenty of attitude!

sewing

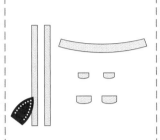

1. Attach the interfacing to the extension, collar, and pocket flaps.

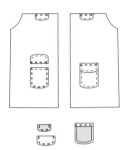

2. With right sides together, sew the pocket flap pieces together, turn them right side out, and top-stitch on the self fabric side (the other side of the flap is in lining fabric). Hem the pockets. Topstitch the pockets and pocket flaps to the front body pieces 2" (5cm) from the center front raw edge; place the lower edge of the patch pockets 3" (7.5cm) up from the bottom raw edge.

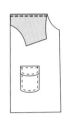

3. With right sides together, sew the front to the front yoke, sandwiching the upper pocket flaps inside.

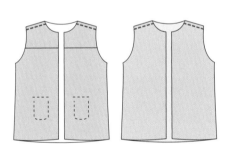

4. With right sides together, sew the front to the back at the shoulders. Do the same for the lining.

5. With right sides together, sew the collar pieces together around the top edge. Turn the collar right side out and topstitch.

sewing

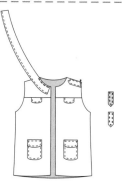

6. With right sides together, sew the collar to the neck-line.

7. With right sides together, sew the epaulettes, turn them right side out, and topstitch. Pin them in place at the shoulder centered on the shoulder seam.

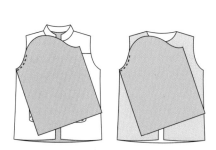

8. With right sides together, sew the sleeves to the armholes. Do the same for the lining.

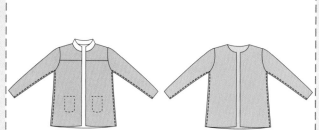

9. With right sides together, sew the front to the back along the side seams from the bottom opening up to the sleeve opening. Do the same for the lining.

10. With right sides together, sew the lining to the body around the neckline, sandwiching the collar.

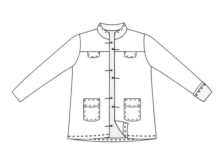

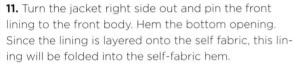

11. Turn the jacket right side out and pin the front lining to the front body. Hem the bottom opening. Since the lining is layered onto the self fabric, this lining will be folded into the self-fabric hem.

12. Hand-stitch the sleeve opening hem to the sleeve opening lining.

13. With right sides together, sew the front extension to the front.

14. Fold the extension in half lengthwise. Also fold back the seam allowance. Topstitch it to the body.

15. Attach the buttons to the front, upper pocket flaps, and epaulettes. Make buttonholes on the front extension and lower pocket flaps only. The front buttonholes and buttons should be spaced evenly between 1" (2.5cm) below the neck and 2" (5cm) above the bottom opening.

CHAPTER 6

THE STRAIGHT COAT

THE BASIC PATTERN WE'LL BE WORKING WITH IN THIS CHAPTER HAS RAGLAN sleeves—an important detail that makes it easily transformable into a whole new range of looks. Because the shoulder seam cuts in across the upper body on the diagonal, the sleeve shape takes on new importance in these projects. It's a fun area to play with volume and contrast—think ruffles, piping, and two-tone fabric choices. The raglan also forms round shoulders, making it an ideal template for softer, slouchier, and sportier looks, like a fluid bell-sleeved kimono, a cozy Baja pullover, or a retro-cute nylon track jacket. With stiffer fabrics, the rounded shape might appear more pronounced, which can give a coat or jacket an avant-garde look.

I've set this basic pattern at knee length—the longest of the three—but as you'll soon discover, that can easily be changed. It comes with a basic collar, too, but remember, the stand-up collar from chapter 4 and the hood from chapter 5 are yours for the taking. The straight body makes it easy to customize, too, whether you're in the mood to add pockets and trim to it, or pump up the volume. So think of these project ideas as starting points, and let your imagination run wild!

kimono chic

With dramatic flared sleeves and a contrast belt, this Asian-inspired wrap jacket lets you be covered up and dressed up. The contrasting effect of black facings and belt against an elegant red-and-black floral-print silk shantung accentuates the lines of the jacket and makes you look long and lean. Wear it after dark to take the chill off an LBD, or over some chic trousers. Add heels and some killer lipstick!

supplies

2 yards (1.8m) red-and-black floral-print silk shantung

1½ yards (1.4m) black silk shantung

1½ yards (1.4m) black fusible interfacing

TRY THESE TOO!

Chic: Natural silk georgette
Hippie: Purple cotton gauze
Fall: Hunter green wool jersey

pattern adjustments

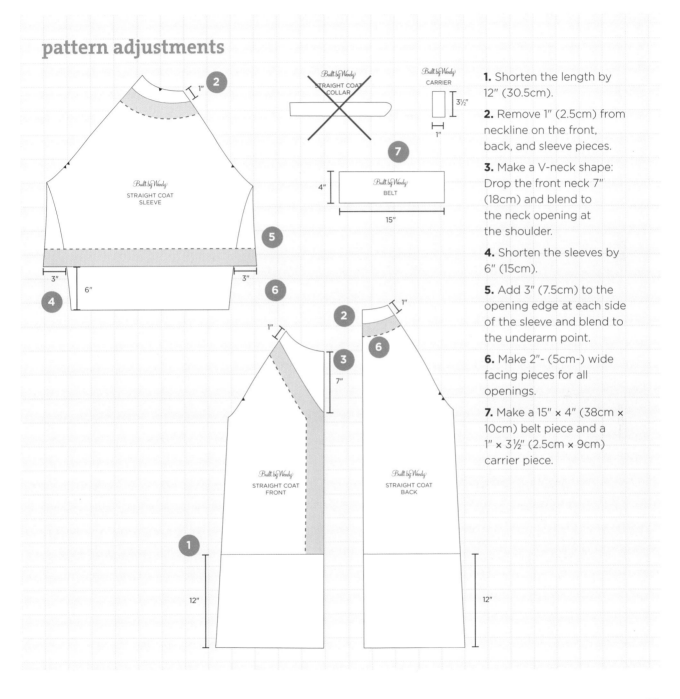

1. Shorten the length by 12″ (30.5cm).

2. Remove 1″ (2.5cm) from neckline on the front, back, and sleeve pieces.

3. Make a V-neck shape: Drop the front neck 7″ (18cm) and blend to the neck opening at the shoulder.

4. Shorten the sleeves by 6″ (15cm).

5. Add 3″ (7.5cm) to the opening edge at each side of the sleeve and blend to the underarm point.

6. Make 2″- (5cm-) wide facing pieces for all openings.

7. Make a 15″ × 4″ (38cm × 10cm) belt piece and a 1″ × 3½″ (2.5cm × 9cm) carrier piece.

pattern adjustments

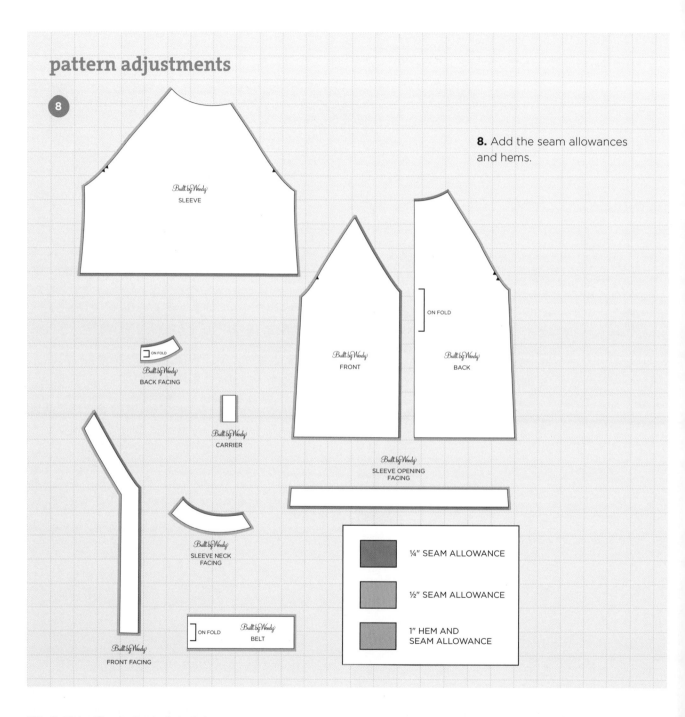

8. Add the seam allowances and hems.

8

Built by Wendy
SLEEVE

ON FOLD
Built by Wendy
BACK FACING

Built by Wendy
CARRIER

Built by Wendy
FRONT

ON FOLD
Built by Wendy
BACK

Built by Wendy
SLEEVE OPENING
FACING

Built by Wendy
SLEEVE NECK
FACING

Built by Wendy
FRONT FACING

ON FOLD
Built by Wendy
BELT

	¼" SEAM ALLOWANCE
	½" SEAM ALLOWANCE
	1" HEM AND SEAM ALLOWANCE

cutting

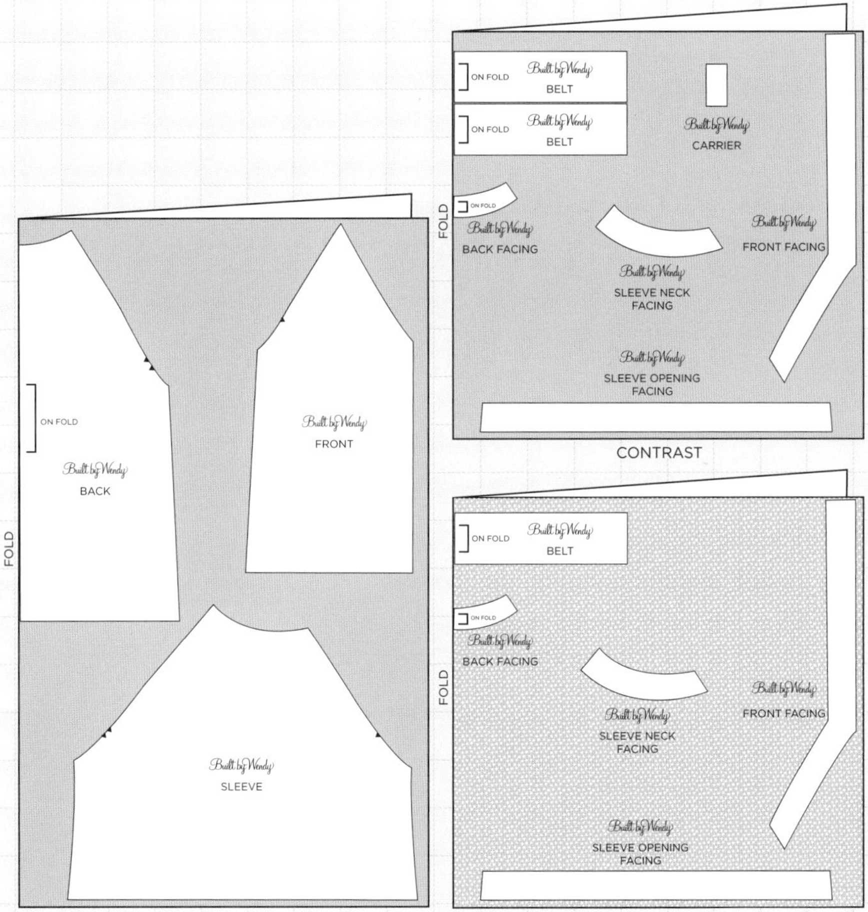
ON FOLD
Built by Wendy
BELT
ON FOLD
Built by Wendy
BELT
Built by Wendy
CARRIER
ON FOLD
FOLD
Built by Wendy
BACK FACING
Built by Wendy
FRONT FACING
Built by Wendy
SLEEVE NECK FACING
Built by Wendy
SLEEVE OPENING FACING
CONTRAST
ON FOLD
Built by Wendy
BACK
FOLD
Built by Wendy
FRONT
Built by Wendy
SLEEVE
ON FOLD
Built by Wendy
BELT
ON FOLD
Built by Wendy
BACK FACING
FOLD
Built by Wendy
FRONT FACING
Built by Wendy
SLEEVE NECK FACING
Built by Wendy
SLEEVE OPENING FACING

Self 44" (112cm)

Contrast 44" (112cm)

Interfacing 44" (112cm)

ALTERNATIVE

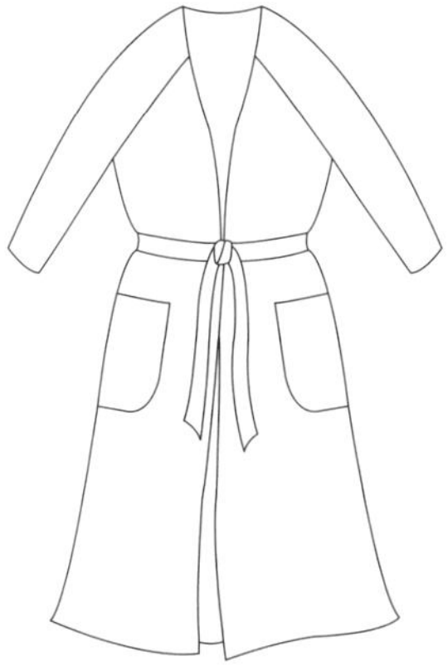

The Soirée Coat

Set at a longer length and whipped up in sumptuous double-faced wool cashmere, this project pattern can make a super-sophisticated coat for special occasions. There's no need for lining, since double-faced cashmere looks and feels equally luxurious inside and out. Keep the sleeves like the original pattern, but add patch pockets for functionality. I can easily picture this over a long column gown with slicked-back hair and some rich, plum-colored fall lipstick.

sewing

1. With right sides together, sew the front body to the front sleeve edges and the back body to the back sleeve edges.

2. Attach the interfacings to the facings and belt. Then with right sides together, sew the neckline facings together (front, sleeve, and back).

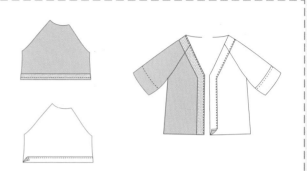

3. With right side to wrong side, sew the sleeve facings to the sleeve openings, turn them right side out, fold back the facing hem, and topstitch. Do the same with the neck and opening facing.

4. With right sides together, sew the front to the back along the side seams from the bottom opening up to the sleeve opening.

5. Hem the bottom opening.

6. Make the belt carriers and attach them to the body. For the placement of the carriers, try on the jacket and mark with a pin where your waist is.

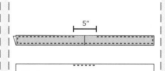

7. Make the belt and thread it through the carriers. See page 78 for sewing belts and carriers.

baja style

This classic hippie pullover doesn't have to be reserved for Mexican vacations or beach bonfires. Using solid gray wool felt instead of the typical stripy weave gives it a cleaner look, bringing the focus to the sporty, casual lines. It makes a great layering piece under a vest, and can even bring a touch of insouciance to a dressier look: Throw it on over a flared skirt with tights, ankle boots, and a statement necklace. Why not?

supplies

2 yards (1.8m) gray wool felt
2 yards (1.8m) gray bias binding

TRY THESE TOO!
Luxe: Gray cashmere
Athletic: Neon yellow nylon with reflec-
    tive stripes
Casual: Navy-and-beige striped cotton

pattern adjustments

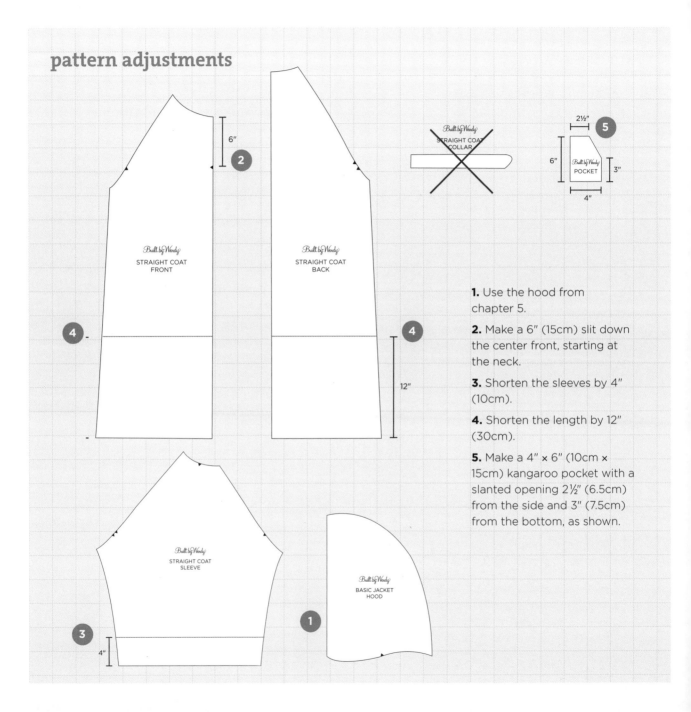

1. Use the hood from chapter 5.

2. Make a 6″ (15cm) slit down the center front, starting at the neck.

3. Shorten the sleeves by 4″ (10cm).

4. Shorten the length by 12″ (30cm).

5. Make a 4″ × 6″ (10cm × 15cm) kangaroo pocket with a slanted opening 2½″ (6.5cm) from the side and 3″ (7.5cm) from the bottom, as shown.

pattern adjustments

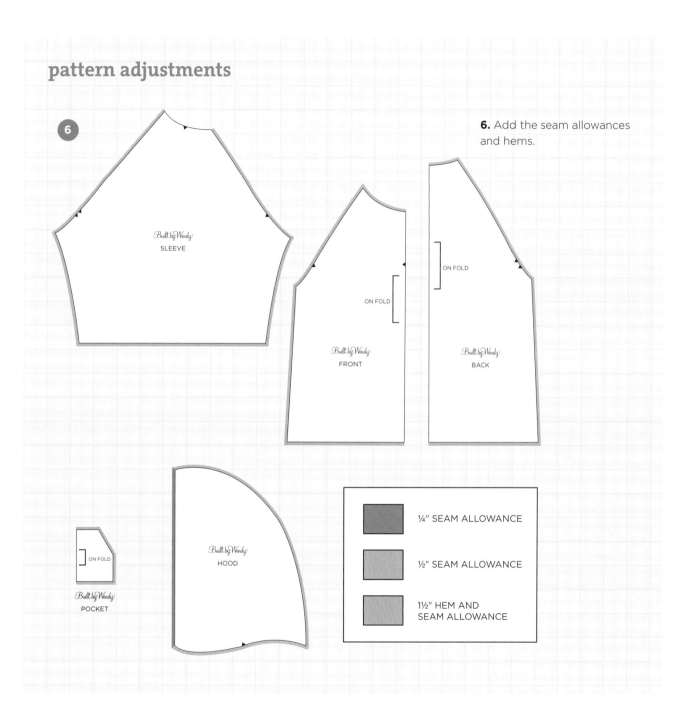

6

6. Add the seam allowances and hems.

Built by Wendy
SLEEVE

Built by Wendy
FRONT

ON FOLD

Built by Wendy
BACK

ON FOLD

Built by Wendy
HOOD

ON FOLD

Built by Wendy
POCKET

¼" SEAM ALLOWANCE

½" SEAM ALLOWANCE

1½" HEM AND
SEAM ALLOWANCE

cutting

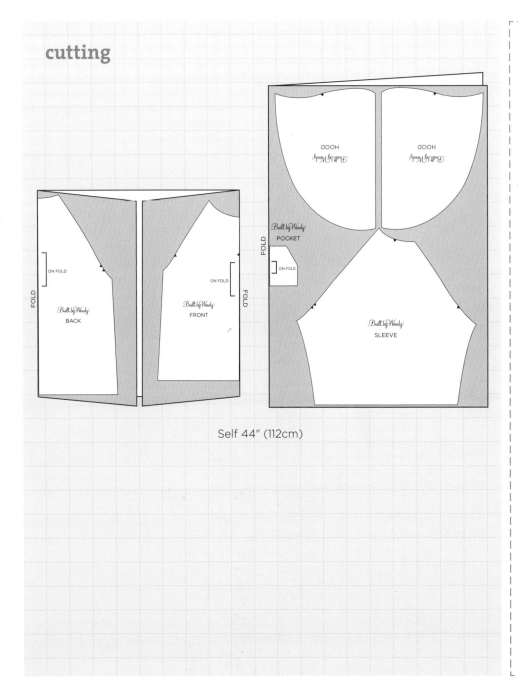

Self 44" (112cm)

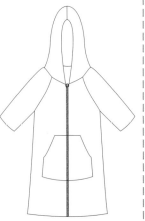

sewing

1. With right sides together, sew the front body to the front sleeve edges and the back body to the back sleeve edges.

2. With right sides together, sew the hood together along the curved edge.

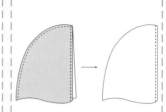

3. With right sides together, sew the hood pieces together around the front. Turn right side out and topstitch around front edge.

4. Sew bias binding around the neck slit.

5. With right sides together, sew the hood to the neckline.

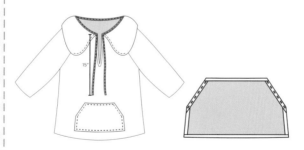

6. Sew bias binding around the neck-hood seam, covering the seam and extending the binding 15″ (38cm) on each side to form a tie.

7. Fold back the pocket openings and topstitch. Topstitch the pocket to the body, placing the bottom edge of the pocket 4″ (10cm) above the bottom opening.

8. With right sides together, sew the front to the back along the side seams from the bottom opening up to the sleeve opening.

9. Hem the openings.

little angel

There's nothing like a statement jacket to put some spring in your step when the seasons change. The wide sleeves on this cropped cotton jacket slenderize the lower body and draw attention to great bracelets and rings, while the brown-and-navy polka-dot print adds a hearty dose of whimsy. This is a perfect layering piece; it gives your basic high-waisted-jeans-and-tank combo plenty of polish, without being too precious.

supplies

2 yards (1.8m) brown-and-navy polka-dot print cotton

½ yard (46cm) black fusible interfacing

4 brown 36 ligne buttons

TRY THESE TOO!

Chic: Brown novelty textured wool

Holiday: Blue velvet

Casual: Indigo denim

pattern adjustments

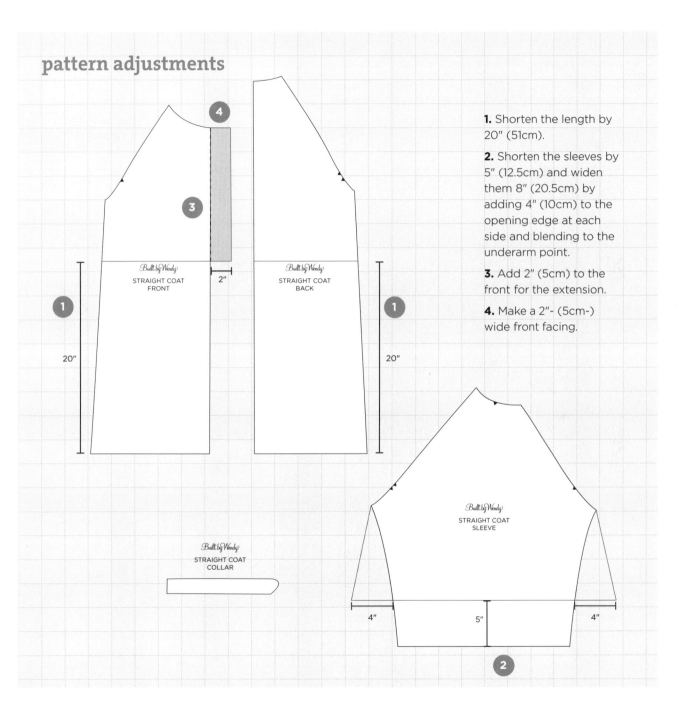

STRAIGHT COAT
FRONT

2"

20"

STRAIGHT COAT
BACK

20"

STRAIGHT COAT
COLLAR

STRAIGHT COAT
SLEEVE

4"   5"   4"

1. Shorten the length by 20" (51cm).

2. Shorten the sleeves by 5" (12.5cm) and widen them 8" (20.5cm) by adding 4" (10cm) to the opening edge at each side and blending to the underarm point.

3. Add 2" (5cm) to the front for the extension.

4. Make a 2"- (5cm-) wide front facing.

pattern adjustments

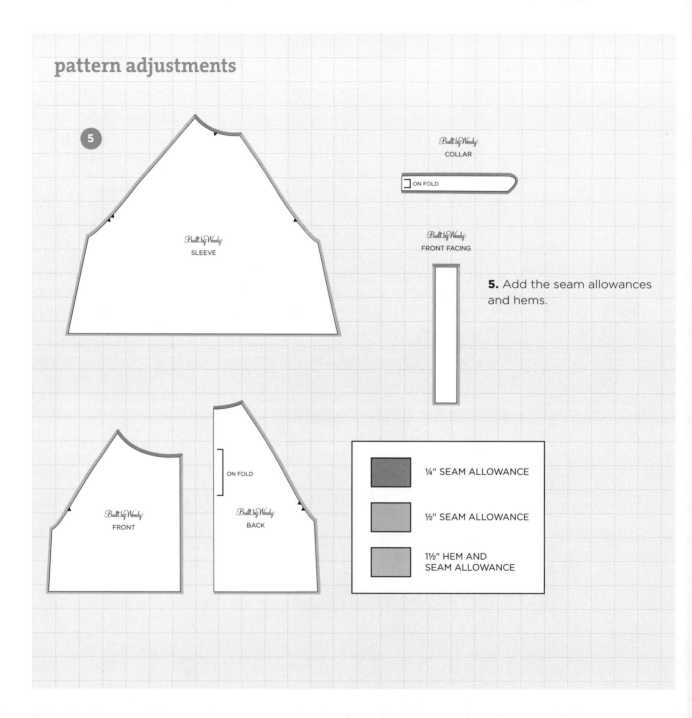

5. Add the seam allowances and hems.

5

SLEEVE
Built by Wendy

COLLAR
Built by Wendy
ON FOLD

FRONT FACING
Built by Wendy

FRONT
Built by Wendy

BACK
Built by Wendy
ON FOLD

¼" SEAM ALLOWANCE

½" SEAM ALLOWANCE

1½" HEM AND
SEAM ALLOWANCE

cutting

Built by Wendy
SLEEVE

Built by Wendy
COLLAR
ON FOLD

Built by Wendy
FRONT FACING

Built by Wendy
COLLAR
ON FOLD

ON FOLD

Built by Wendy
BACK

Built by Wendy
FRONT

FOLD

Self 44" (112cm)

Built by Wendy
COLLAR
ON FOLD

Built by Wendy
FRONT FACING

FOLD

Interfacing 44" (112cm)

Puff the Magic Jacket

This chic little accent adds a bit of French flavor to a basic shell vest. Shorten sleeves just shy of the armhole, slash and spread the sleeve at the neckline to add room for gathering, and curve the front bottom opening a bit. I love it in a bright Ultrasuede or a dark wool tweed for cooler weather; for spring, try it in cotton canvas. So simple and chic, you may just wear it on its own as a top!

sewing

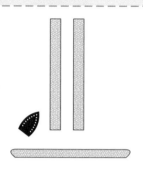

1. Attach the interfacing to the front facing and collar.

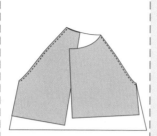

2. With right sides together, sew the front body to the front sleeve edges and the back body to the back sleeve edges.

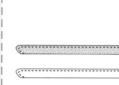

3. With right sides together, sew the collar pieces together around the outer edge and sides. Turn right side out and topstitch.

4. With right sides together, sew the collar to the neckline beginning at the center backs.

5. With right sides together, sew the front to the back along the side seams from the bottom opening up to the sleeve opening.

6. With right sides together, sew the front facing to the neck, front, and bottom opening. Turn it right side out and understitch.

7. Hem the openings.

8. Attach the buttons and make the buttonholes, spacing them evenly between 1" (2.5cm) below the neck and 2" (5cm) above the bottom opening.

PROJECT 4

da bomber

Who doesn't love a fun little bomber to throw on over everything and stash in your suitcase for impromptu weekend getaways? The difference with mine is that you can tailor it to fit you perfectly—no more ballooning sides or too-short arms! It's a fun shape for playing with fabrics. This version comes in fresh navy-and-purple madras plaid, making it a spiffy spring staple for pairing with tailored shorts or a cutoff denim mini.

supplies

2 yards (1.8m) navy-and-purple cotton madras plaid

½ yard (46cm) black fusible interfacing

2 yards (1.8m) of 1½"- (3.8cm-) wide black elastic

22" (56cm) navy plastic separating zipper

TRY THESE TOO!
Chic: Black silk georgette
Preppy: White cotton piqué
Casual: Royal blue linen

pattern adjustments

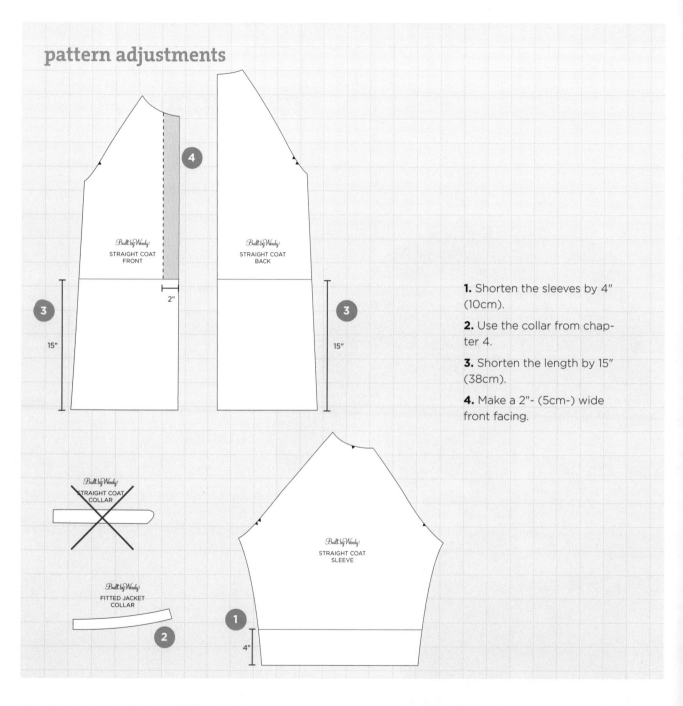

STRAIGHT COAT
FRONT

2"

STRAIGHT COAT
BACK

15"

15"

STRAIGHT COAT
COLLAR

FITTED JACKET
COLLAR

STRAIGHT COAT
SLEEVE

4"

1. Shorten the sleeves by 4" (10cm).

2. Use the collar from chapter 4.

3. Shorten the length by 15" (38cm).

4. Make a 2"- (5cm-) wide front facing.

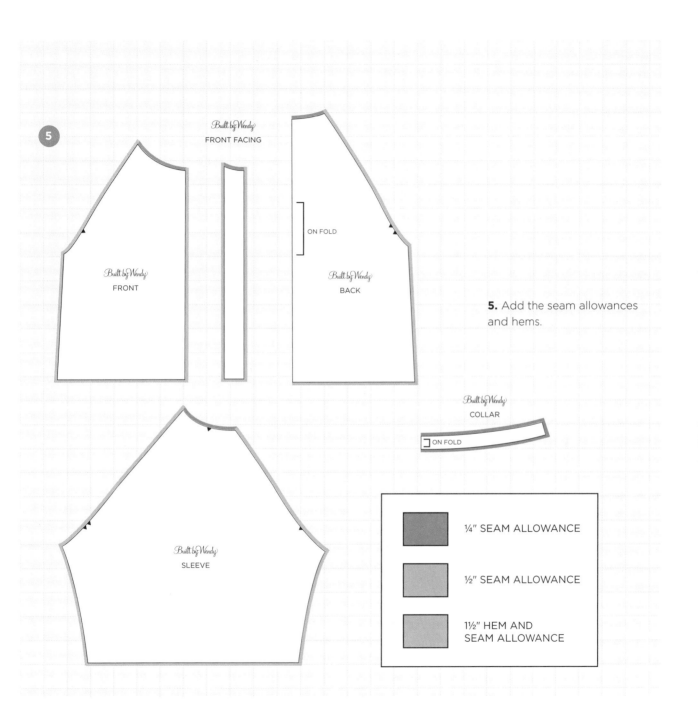

5

Built by Wendy
FRONT FACING

Built by Wendy
FRONT

Built by Wendy
BACK

ON FOLD

5. Add the seam allowances and hems.

Built by Wendy
COLLAR

ON FOLD

Built by Wendy
SLEEVE

■	¼" SEAM ALLOWANCE
■	½" SEAM ALLOWANCE
■	1½" HEM AND SEAM ALLOWANCE

cutting

Self 44" (112cm)

- Built by Wendy FRONT FACING
- ON FOLD
- Built by Wendy BACK
- Built by Wendy FRONT
- FOLD
- Built by Wendy COLLAR — ON FOLD
- Built by Wendy COLLAR — ON FOLD
- Built by Wendy SLEEVE

Interfacing 44" (112cm)

- FOLD
- Built by Wendy COLLAR — ON FOLD
- Built by Wendy FRONT FACING
- **INTERFACING**

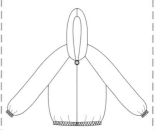

ALTERNATIVE

Track Star

Whether you're training for a marathon or just running all over town, a sporty nylon track jacket is a light, effortless essential. I love it as an alternative to a leather bomber or as a just-in-case piece to toss in your bag when the forecast calls for rain. Why not make it in several bright colors? Just don't forget that nylon needs extra precaution when pressing, and use nonfusible interfacing!

sewing

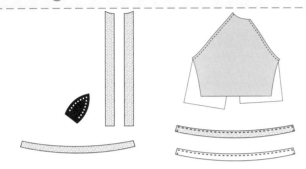

1. Attach interfacing to the front facings and collar.

2. With right sides together, sew the front body to the front sleeve edges and the back body to the back sleeve edges.

3. With right sides together, sew the collar pieces together around the outer edge and sides. Turn it right side out and topstitch.

4. With right sides together, sew the collar to the neckline beginning at the center back.

5. Attach the zipper at the center front starting with teeth 3/4" (2cm) down from the neck and ending 1" (2.5cm) above the bottom opening's raw edge.

6. With right sides together, sew the front facing to the neck. Turn it right side out, fold back the front seam allowance, and hand-stitch the facing's front edge to the zipper tape inside the garment.

7. Hem the sleeve opening and insert the elastic inside of the hem. Pin the elastic to each opening so it doesn't slip inside of the hem tunnel.

8. With right sides together, sew the front to the back along the side seams from the bottom opening up to the sleeve opening, securing the ends of the elastic in the sleeve hem as you sew the hem closed.

9. Hem the bottom opening and insert the elastic inside of the hem. Stitch the center front along the zipper topstitch line a few inches (5cm–10cm) to secure the elastic and close the front opening.

army of one

This classic everyday-casual piece is the perfect way to arm yourself for everyday adventures. It has a classic collar and oversized-pocket and shoulder-yoke details, and unlike your musty Vietnam-era version, it's tailored to a woman's body. That means you'll always feel put together in it, whether you slip it atop a sundress for a rock festival or take it Parisian chic for an afternoon of shopping with a big scarf and black tights.

supplies

3 yards (2.7m) olive cotton ripstop
¾ yard (69cm) black fusible interfacing
13 olive 36 ligne buttons

TRY THESE TOO!
Chic: Taupe silk-wool blend
Rain: Brown water-repellent ripstop
Fall: Gray wool felt

pattern adjustments

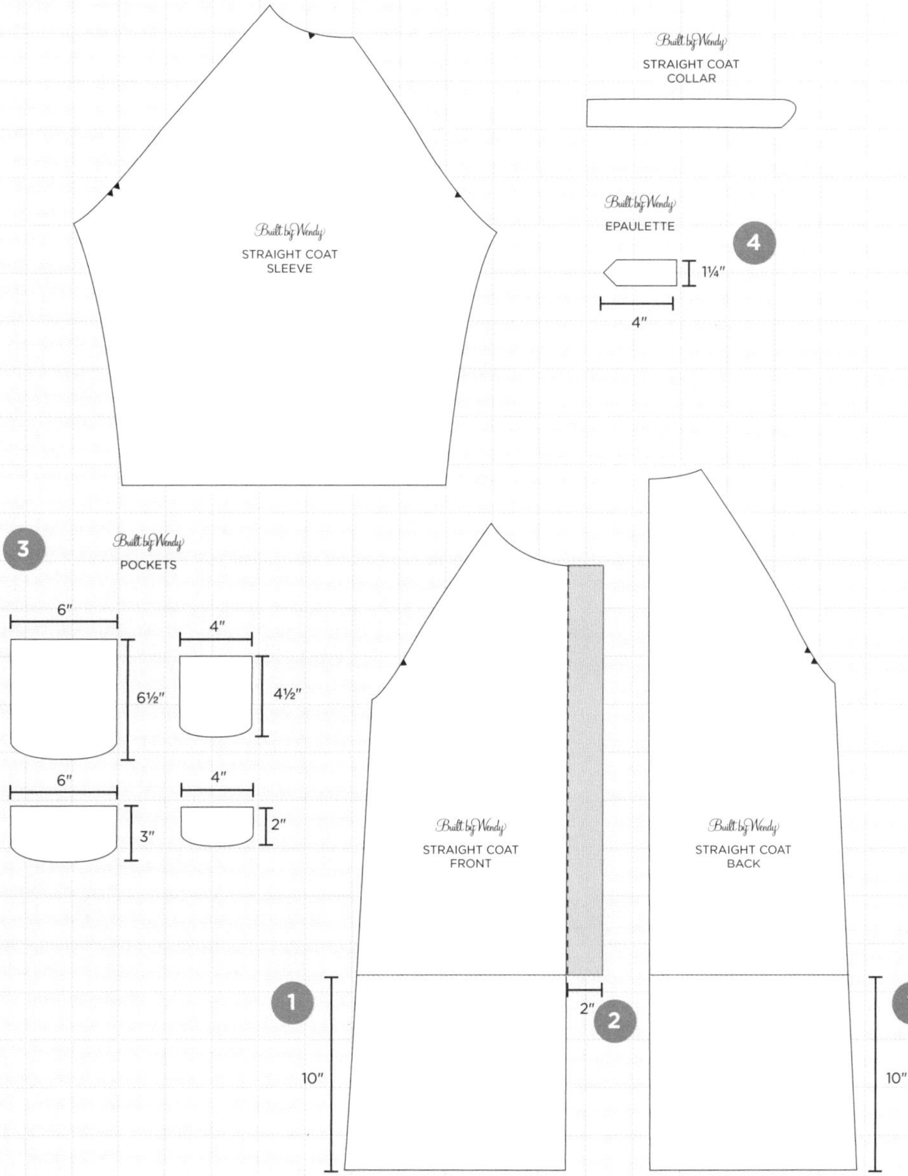

Built by Wendy
STRAIGHT COAT
COLLAR

Built by Wendy
STRAIGHT COAT
SLEEVE

Built by Wendy
EPAULETTE

4

1¼"

4"

3

Built by Wendy
POCKETS

6"

6½"

4"

4½"

6"

3"

4"

2"

Built by Wendy
STRAIGHT COAT
FRONT

Built by Wendy
STRAIGHT COAT
BACK

1

2

2"

10"

1

10"

1. Shorten the length by 10" (25cm).

2. Add 2" (5cm) to the front for the extension. Make a 2" (5cm) front facing.

3. Make a 6" × 6½" (15cm × 16.5cm) pocket with a 6" × 3" (15cm × 7.5cm) flap, and a 4" × 4½" (10cm × 11.5cm) pocket with a 4" × 2" (10cm × 5cm) flap, rounding the bottoms of all 4 pieces.

4. Make 4" × 1¼" (10cm × 3cm) sleeve and shoulder epaulettes with one end pointed.

pattern adjustments

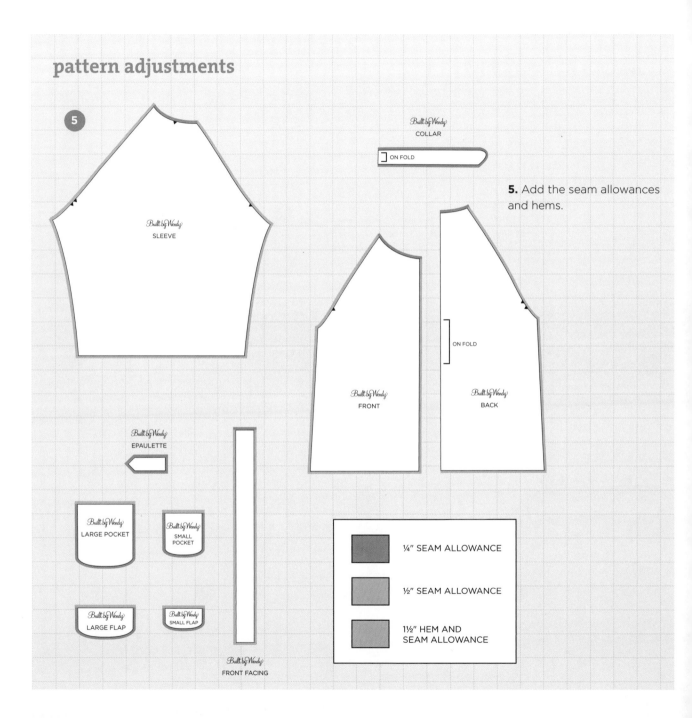

5

Built by Wendy
SLEEVE

Built by Wendy
COLLAR

ON FOLD

5. Add the seam allowances and hems.

Built by Wendy
FRONT

Built by Wendy
BACK

ON FOLD

Built by Wendy
EPAULETTE

Built by Wendy
LARGE POCKET

Built by Wendy
SMALL POCKET

Built by Wendy
LARGE FLAP

Built by Wendy
SMALL FLAP

Built by Wendy
FRONT FACING

	¼" SEAM ALLOWANCE
	½" SEAM ALLOWANCE
	1½" HEM AND SEAM ALLOWANCE

cutting

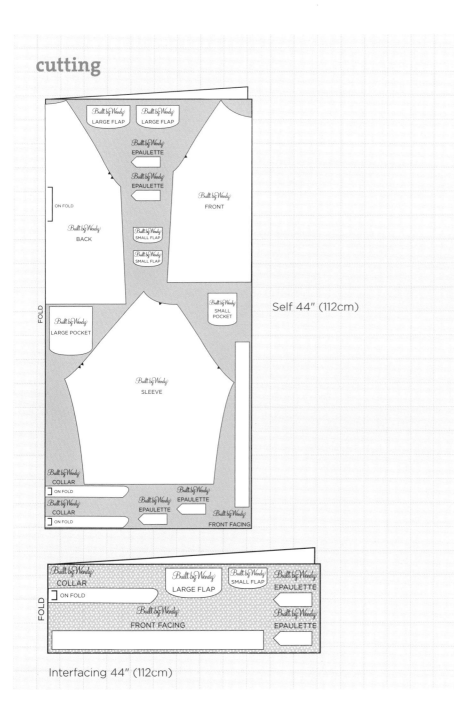

Self 44" (112cm)

Interfacing 44" (112cm)

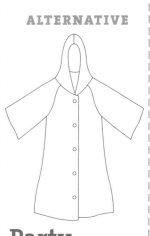

sewing

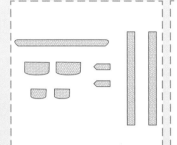

1. Attach interfacing to the collar, front facings, epaulettes, and pocket flaps.

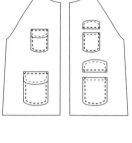

2. With right sides together, sew the pocket flaps together, turn them right side out and top-stitch. Sew the pockets and flaps to the front pieces. Place the bottom of the large lower pocket 2" (5cm) above the raw edge and place the small pocket flap's top edge 3" (7.5cm) down from the neck. All pockets should be placed 3" (7.5cm) in from the center front raw edge.

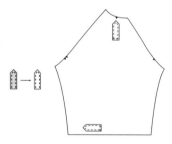

3. With right sides together, sew the epaulette pieces together, turn them right side out, and topstitch. Then sew them to the sleeves at the square ends. Center each piece on the sleeve and place the epaulette point towards the back of the sleeve 1½" (3.8cm) above the sleeve opening. For the shoulder epaulette, place it on the sleeve's center with the pointed end 1" (2.5cm) below the sleeve neckline.

4. With right sides together, sew the front body to the front sleeve edges and the back body to the back sleeve edges.

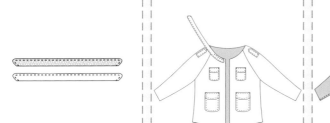

5. With right sides together, sew the collar pieces together around the outer edge and sides. Turn it right side out and topstitch.

6. With right sides together, sew the collar to the neckline beginning at the center back.

7. With right sides together, sew the front to the back along the side seams from the bottom opening up to the sleeve opening.

8. With right sides together, sew the front facing to the neck, front, and bottom opening. Turn it right side out and understitch.

9. Hem the openings.

10. Attach the buttons and make the buttonholes, spacing them equally 1" (2.5cm) below the neck and 2" (5cm) above the bottom opening. For the buttons on the epaulettes, place them in the pointed area as shown on the illustration. Center the pocket buttons and buttonholes 1" (2.5cm) from the pocket flap edge and pocket hem.

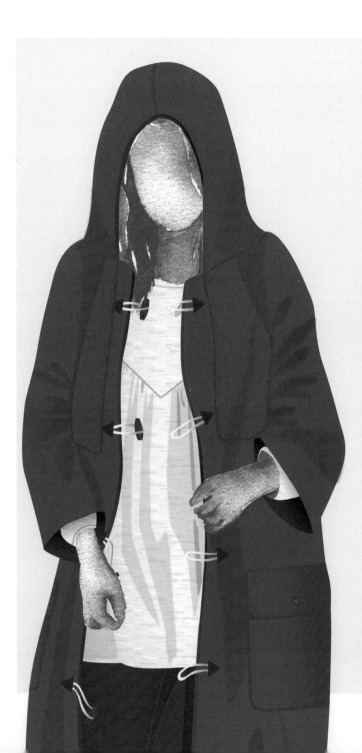

the paddington coat

This classic silhouette evokes Paddington Bear, the English countryside, and Ali MacGraw in *Love Story*. What's not to love? The oversized wooden toggles make a strong style statement, as does the bright red hue. Cozy boiled wool has plenty of body, giving the coat a rich-looking texture and dimension. It's the ideal outer layer for rustic, ladylike looks (think tweed skirts, hunting boots, and Aran sweaters).

supplies

4 yards (3.7m) red boiled wool
½ yard (46cm) black fusible interfacing
4 toggle sets
2 red 32 ligne buttons

TRY THESE TOO!
Rustic: Brown wool tweed
Summer: Pale green cotton canvas
Chic: Black leatherette

pattern adjustments

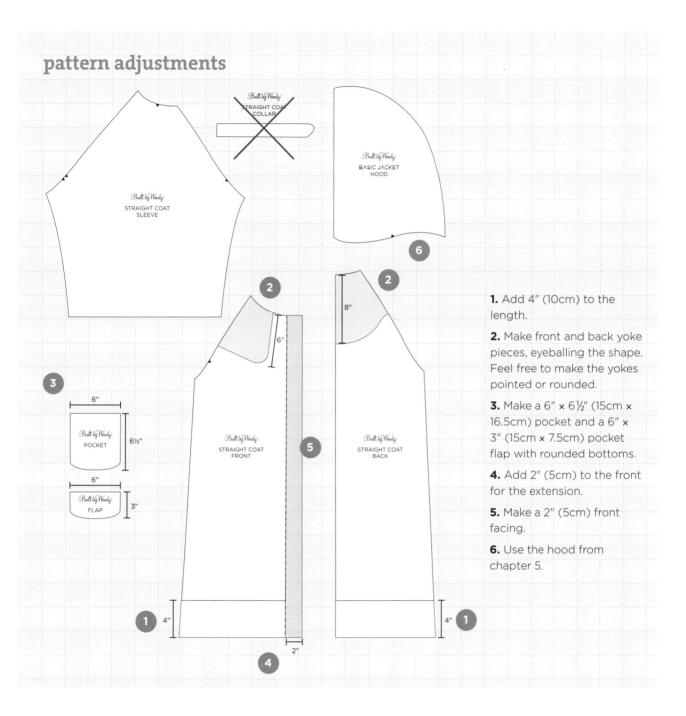

1. Add 4″ (10cm) to the length.

2. Make front and back yoke pieces, eyeballing the shape. Feel free to make the yokes pointed or rounded.

3. Make a 6″ × 6½″ (15cm × 16.5cm) pocket and a 6″ × 3″ (15cm × 7.5cm) pocket flap with rounded bottoms.

4. Add 2″ (5cm) to the front for the extension.

5. Make a 2″ (5cm) front facing.

6. Use the hood from chapter 5.

pattern adjustments

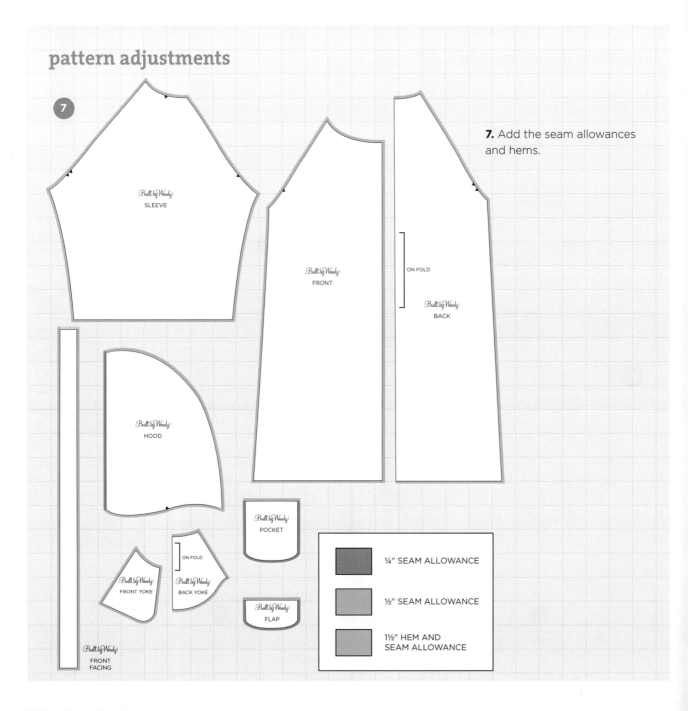

Built by Wendy
SLEEVE

Built by Wendy
FRONT

ON FOLD

Built by Wendy
BACK

7. Add the seam allowances and hems.

Built by Wendy
HOOD

Built by Wendy
POCKET

Built by Wendy
FRONT YOKE

ON FOLD

Built by Wendy
BACK YOKE

Built by Wendy
FLAP

Built by Wendy
FRONT FACING

■	¼" SEAM ALLOWANCE
■	½" SEAM ALLOWANCE
■	1½" HEM AND SEAM ALLOWANCE

cutting

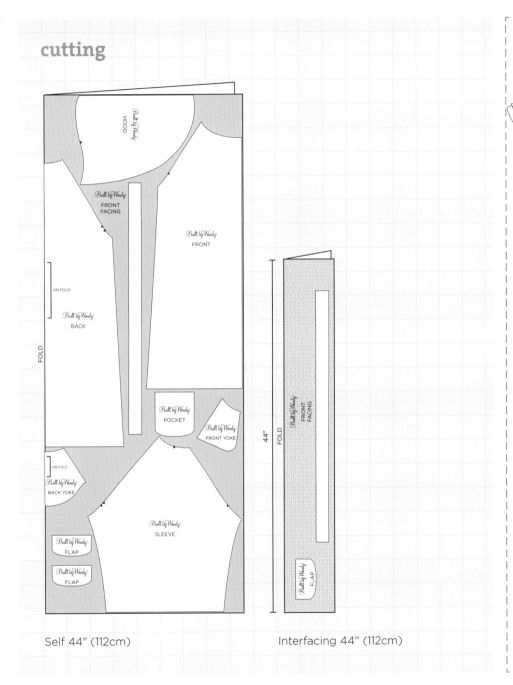

HOOD

Built by Wendy

FRONT FACING

Built by Wendy

FRONT

Built by Wendy

ON FOLD

BACK

Built by Wendy

FOLD

POCKET

Built by Wendy

FRONT YOKE

Built by Wendy

ON FOLD

BACK YOKE

Built by Wendy

SLEEVE

Built by Wendy

FLAP

Built by Wendy

FLAP

Built by Wendy

Self 44" (112cm)

FOLD

44"

FRONT FACING

Built by Wendy

FLAP

Built by Wendy

Interfacing 44" (112cm)

ALTERNATIVE

Trench Connection

Toggles look equally chic against water-repellent khaki twill. You can also try the same fabric in navy or olive for a subtle twist on the classic. Try playing with lining, too; you can go with the timeless plaid wool or even an unexpected bright color. Add a belt and carriers and the hood from chapter 5 for an all-weather topper that's elegant enough for lunch at the Mayfair. Inspector Gadget never had it this good!

sewing

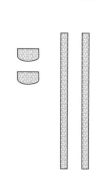

1. Attach the interfacing to the front facings and pocket flaps.

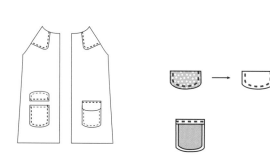

2. With right sides together, sew the pocket flap pieces together, turn right side out, and topstitch. Hem the pockets. Sew the pockets and flaps to the front pieces.

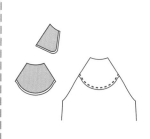

3. Fold back the yoke hems. Topstitch the front yokes to the front and the back yokes to the back.

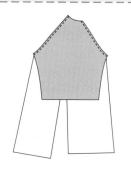

4. With right sides together, sew the front body to the front sleeve edges and the back body to the back sleeve edges.

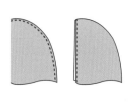

5. With right sides together, sew the hood pieces along the curved edge.

6. With right sides together, sew the hood pieces together around the front. Then turn right side out.

7. With right sides together, sew the hood to the neckline beginning at the center back points.

8. With right sides together, sew the front to the back along the side seams from the bottom opening up to the sleeve opening.

9. With right sides together, sew the front facing to the neck, front, and bottom opening. Turn it right side out and understitch.

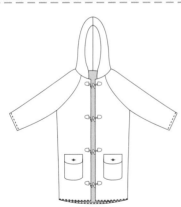

10. Hem the openings.

11. Attach the toggles to the front, spacing them 4″ (10cm) apart starting at 1″ (2.5cm) below the neck. Attach buttons to the pockets and make buttonholes on the pocket flaps.

the scarf coat

I love garments that do double duty. This wool-cashmere knockout has an extended neck piece that wraps around you and ties in front, like a scarf and a coat in one! It makes an otherwise simple silhouette more interesting and fancy, and, of course, it also keeps your neck warm. Since the scarf piece will brush against your skin, be sure not to skimp on the fabric.

supplies

2½ yards (2.3m) black wool cashmere
1 yard (91cm) black fusible interfacing
¼ yard (23cm) black lining
6 black 36 ligne buttons

TRY THESE TOO!

Chic: White silk-wool blend
Rain: Navy water-repellent canvas
Casual: Black cotton twill

pattern adjustments

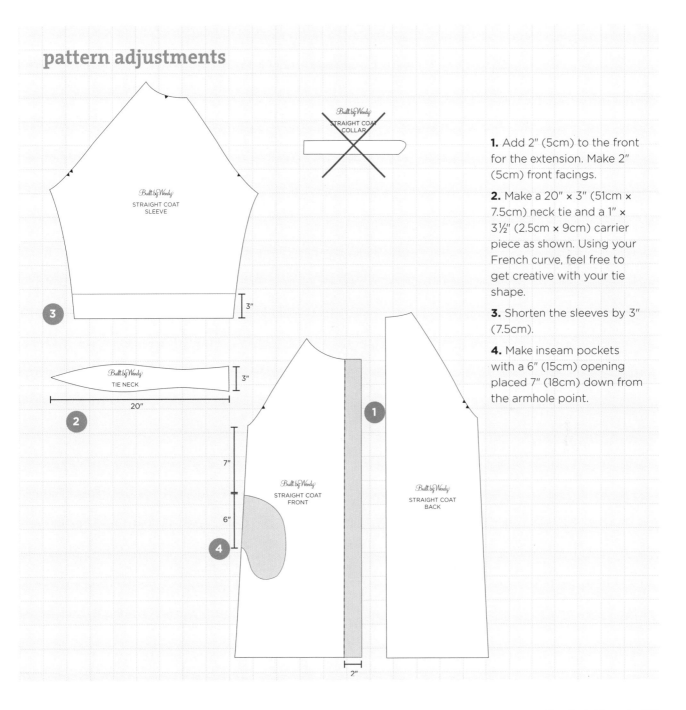

Built by Wendy
STRAIGHT COAT
SLEEVE

Built by Wendy
STRAIGHT COAT
COLLAR

Built by Wendy
TIE NECK

20"

3"

Built by Wendy
STRAIGHT COAT
FRONT

Built by Wendy
STRAIGHT COAT
BACK

7"

6"

2"

3"

1. Add 2″ (5cm) to the front for the extension. Make 2″ (5cm) front facings.

2. Make a 20″ × 3″ (51cm × 7.5cm) neck tie and a 1″ × 3½″ (2.5cm × 9cm) carrier piece as shown. Using your French curve, feel free to get creative with your tie shape.

3. Shorten the sleeves by 3″ (7.5cm).

4. Make inseam pockets with a 6″ (15cm) opening placed 7″ (18cm) down from the armhole point.

pattern adjustments

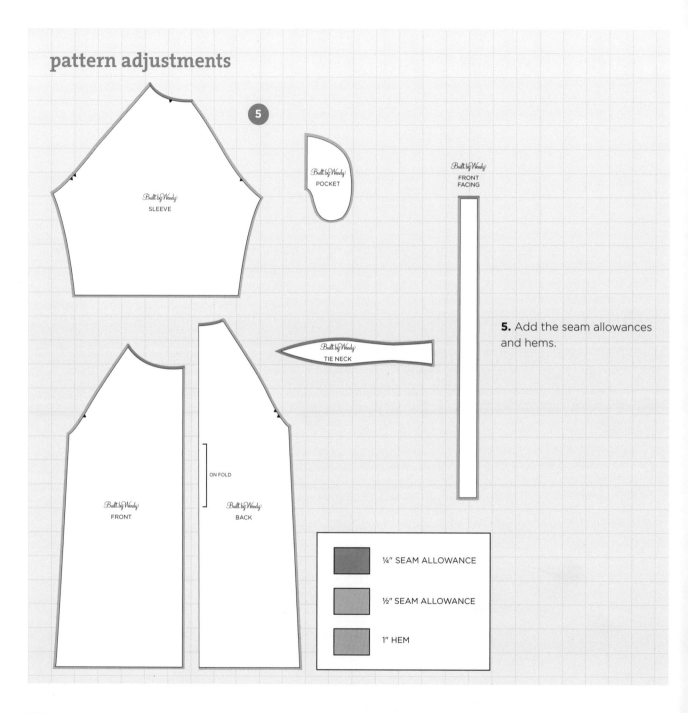

5

Built by Wendy
SLEEVE

Built by Wendy
POCKET

Built by Wendy
FRONT
FACING

Built by Wendy
TIE NECK

5. Add the seam allowances and hems.

ON FOLD

Built by Wendy
FRONT

Built by Wendy
BACK

¼" SEAM ALLOWANCE

½" SEAM ALLOWANCE

1" HEM

cutting

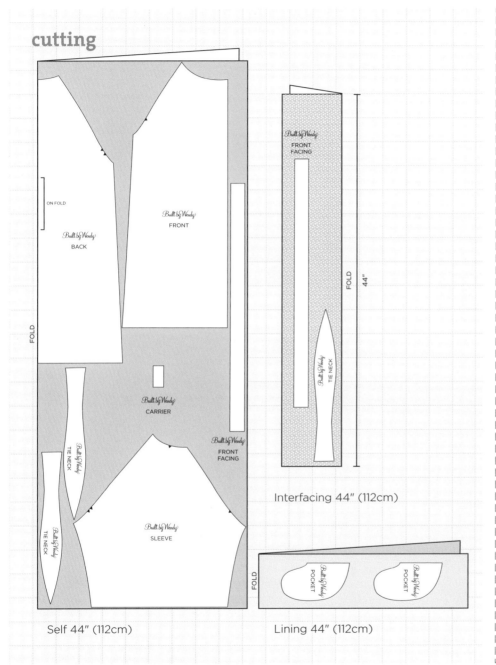

ON FOLD

Built by Wendy
BACK

Built by Wendy
FRONT

FOLD

Built by Wendy
CARRIER

Built by Wendy
TIE NECK

Built by Wendy
TIE NECK

Built by Wendy
SLEEVE

Built by Wendy
FRONT FACING

FOLD

Self 44" (112cm)

Built by Wendy
FRONT FACING

FOLD

44"

Built by Wendy
TIE NECK

Interfacing 44" (112cm)

FOLD

Built by Wendy
POCKET

Built by Wendy
POCKET

Lining 44" (112cm)

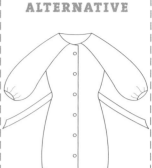

Fit to Be Tied

The same simple silhouette can be adapted into this elegant evening alternative. It's a guaranteed head turner for a night at the theatre! Shorten the sleeves to three-quarter length and insert elastic into the ends to create a gathered shape. Make ties to attach at the waist and knot them in a bow in the back; this will contour the shape at your waist and create a dramatic exit. To keep the emphasis there, skip the tie neck and go collarless.

sewing

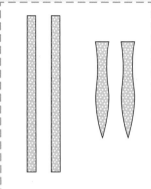

1. Attach interfacing to the front facing and neck tie.

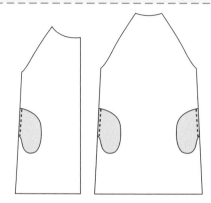

2. With right sides together, sew the pockets to the front and back.

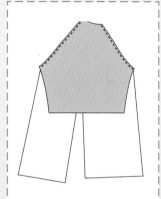

3. With right sides together, sew the front body to the front sleeve edges and the back body to the back sleeve edges.

4. With right sides together, sew the front facing to the front pieces and bottom opening. Turn it right side out and understitch.

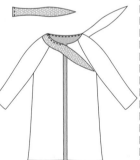

5. With right sides together, sew the neck-ties halves together. Sew one piece to the neckline beginning at the center back points.

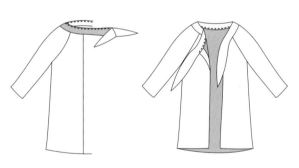

6. With right sides together, sew the necktie to the necktie facing around top edge and sew the pointed extensions around to the center front neck. Turn it right side out, fold back the tie-facing neckline seam allowance, and hand-stitch the remaining opening to the neckline seam.

7. With right sides together, sew the front to the back along the side seams from the bottom opening up to the sleeve opening, sewing around the inseam pockets.

8. Hem the openings.

9. Attach the buttons and make the buttonholes, spacing them equally between 1" (2.5cm) below the neck and 5" (12.5cm) above the bottom opening.

10. Make a buttonhole 1½" (3.8cm) tall on the right front tie just above the buttonhole. Slip the left side of the front tie through the buttonhole, then tie the necktie in a knot.

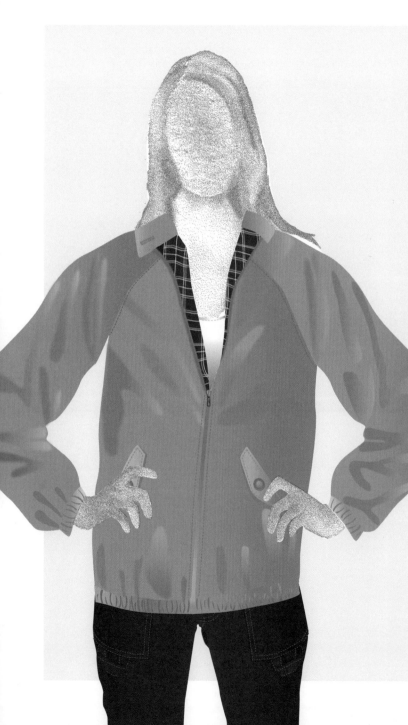

tee time

Even if the closest you get to the golf course is an occasional round of putt-putt, it's easy to enjoy the cute, tomboyish charm of a golf jacket. This one, in khaki cotton twill, is anything but par for the course. Fitted for the female figure, it has a tab collar, zip front, and plaid lining for a touch of sass. It's easy to style in a city-chic way: Try it with a chambray button-down, miniskirt, and ballet flats.

supplies

2 yards (1.8m) khaki cotton twill
2 yards (1.8m) red plaid cotton shirting
1 yard (91cm) white fusible interfacing
1½ yards (1.4m) of 1"- (2.5cm-) wide elastic
3 khaki 24 ligne buttons
20" silver separating zipper

TRY THESE!
Rain: Red water-repellent twill
Sporty: Acid green nylon
Chic: Gray wool tweed

pattern adjustments

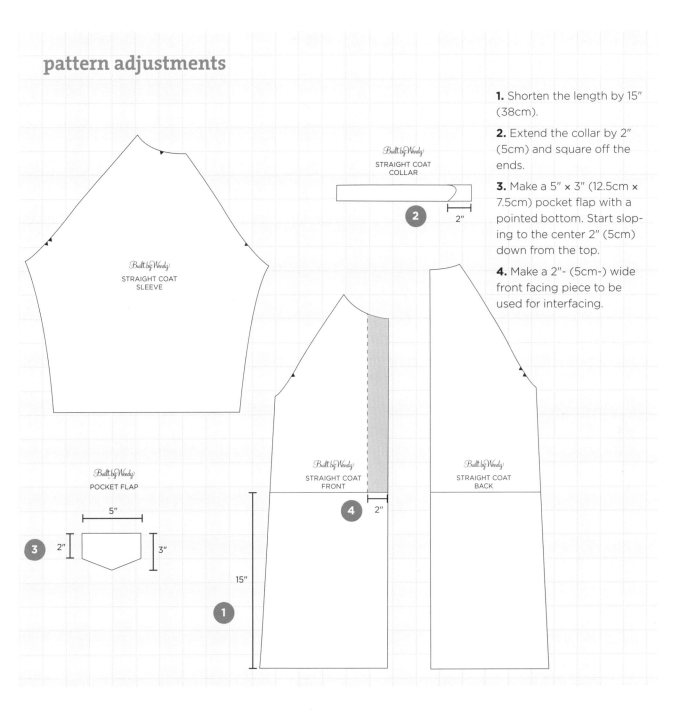

1. Shorten the length by 15″ (38cm).

2. Extend the collar by 2″ (5cm) and square off the ends.

3. Make a 5″ × 3″ (12.5cm × 7.5cm) pocket flap with a pointed bottom. Start sloping to the center 2″ (5cm) down from the top.

4. Make a 2″- (5cm-) wide front facing piece to be used for interfacing.

Built by Wendy
STRAIGHT COAT
SLEEVE

Built by Wendy
STRAIGHT COAT
COLLAR

2″

Built by Wendy
POCKET FLAP

5″

2″ 3″

Built by Wendy
STRAIGHT COAT
FRONT

2″

Built by Wendy
STRAIGHT COAT
BACK

15″

pattern adjustments

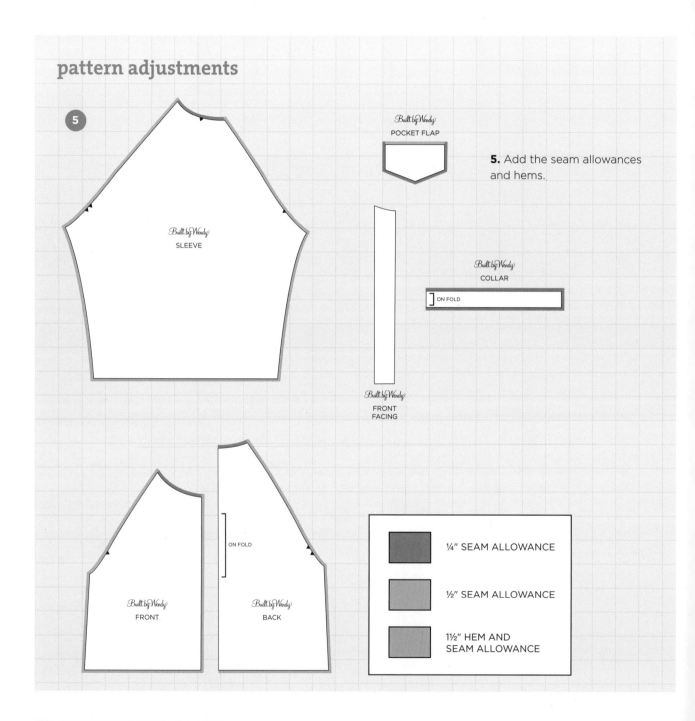

5

Built by Wendy
POCKET FLAP

5. Add the seam allowances and hems.

Built by Wendy
SLEEVE

Built by Wendy
COLLAR

ON FOLD

Built by Wendy
FRONT FACING

ON FOLD

Built by Wendy
FRONT

Built by Wendy
BACK

ON FOLD

¼" SEAM ALLOWANCE

½" SEAM ALLOWANCE

1½" HEM AND SEAM ALLOWANCE

cutting

BACK — *Built by Wendy* — ON FOLD

FRONT — *Built by Wendy*

SLEEVE — *Built by Wendy*

FOLD

LINING

COLLAR — *Built by Wendy* — ON FOLD

POCKET FLAP — *Built by Wendy*

FRONT FACING — *Built by Wendy*

FOLD

Lining 44" (112cm)

Interfacing 44" (112cm)

BACK — *Built by Wendy* — ON FOLD

FRONT — *Built by Wendy*

POCKET FLAP — *Built by Wendy*

POCKET FLAP — *Built by Wendy*

SLEEVE — *Built by Wendy*

COLLAR — *Built by Wendy* — ON FOLD
ON FOLD

COLLAR — *Built by Wendy*

FOLD

Self 44" (112cm)

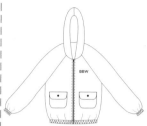

The Varsity Jacket

Lettermen's jackets have a fun, retro vibe that's easy to throw on—and when you make your own with this pattern, it will fit way better than your sophomore-year boyfriend's version ever did! Just make the body in wool felt and the sleeves in leatherette, and add the hood from chapter 5. You can even add an iron-on appliqué monogram to make it authentic. Why not choose your own initials?

sewing

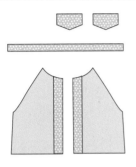

1. Attach interfacing to the front lining, pocket flaps, and collar.

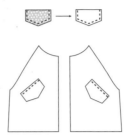

2. With right sides together, sew the pocket flap pieces together, turn them right side out, and top-stitch. Sew the pocket flaps to the front pieces, placing the pocket flap's top point 4" (10cm) above the raw bottom edge and 3" (7.5cm) in from the front edge. Angle the flap down by 1" (2.5cm) at the side seam side. See the illustration for positioning.

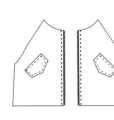

3. Attach the zipper on the center front, placing the teeth 1" (2.5cm) from the neck and finishing at 1½" (3.8cm) above the bottom raw edge.

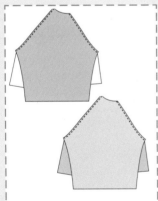

4. With right sides together, sew the front body to the front sleeve edges and the back body to the back sleeve edges. Do the same for the lining.

5. With right sides together, sew the front to the back along the side seams from the bottom opening up to the sleeve opening. Do the same for the lining.

6. Hand-stitch the lining front to the zipper tape. With wrong sides together, pin the lining necklines, bottom, and sleeve openings to the body.

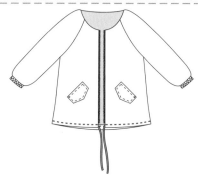

7. Hem the sleeve opening, leaving a 2" (5cm) opening. Insert a 6" (15cm) length of elastic inside of the hem. Join the elastic ends together, then topstitch the sleeve opening closed. Do the same for the other sleeve opening.

8. Hem the bottom opening and insert a 33" (84cm) length of elastic inside of the hem. Stitch the center front along the zipper topstitch line for a few inches (5cm–10cm) to secure the elastic and close the front opening.

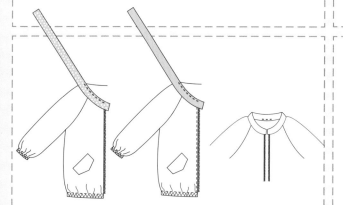

9. With right sides together, sew the collar to the neckline beginning at the center back.

10. With right sides together, sew the collar to the collar facing, leaving 2" (5cm) open at the center back. Turn right side out and hand-stitch the opening closed.

11. Attach buttons onto the pocket flaps 1" (2.5cm) above the bottom edge, centered and sewn through both the pocket flap and garment body. Attach collar button and make a buttonhole centered on the opposite side of the collar above the zipper.

the two-tone coat

The idea behind this coat may be super simple, but the effect will cause double takes everywhere you go! The coat uses wool felt in navy on the body and gray on the yoke and collar. vThe effect is a little bit mod without feeling retro. Play up the contrast with a solid-colored scarf and tights, or just throw it on over your favorite old jeans to give an everyday outfit some extra je ne sais quoi.

supplies

1½ yards (1.4m) navy wool felt

1 yard (91cm) gray wool felt

½ yard navy lining

1 yard (91cm) black fusible interfacing

5 navy buttons

TRY THESE TOO!

Rain: Black-and-khaki color-blocked water-repellent canvas

Fall: Black wool tweed with brown faux-fur yoke

Preppy: Navy wool with plaid piping inserted along the yoke seam

pattern adjustments

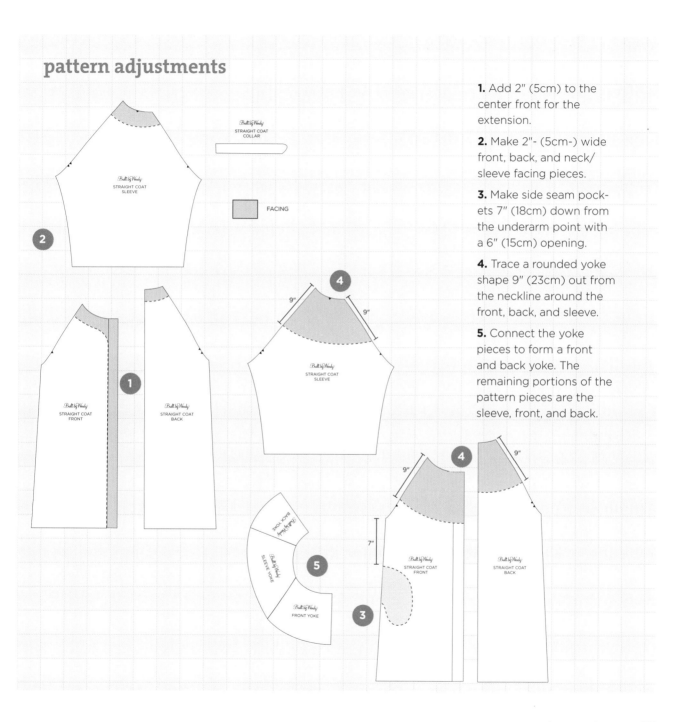

1. Add 2" (5cm) to the center front for the extension.

2. Make 2"- (5cm-) wide front, back, and neck/sleeve facing pieces.

3. Make side seam pockets 7" (18cm) down from the underarm point with a 6" (15cm) opening.

4. Trace a rounded yoke shape 9" (23cm) out from the neckline around the front, back, and sleeve.

5. Connect the yoke pieces to form a front and back yoke. The remaining portions of the pattern pieces are the sleeve, front, and back.

pattern adjustments

6. Add the seam allowances and hems.

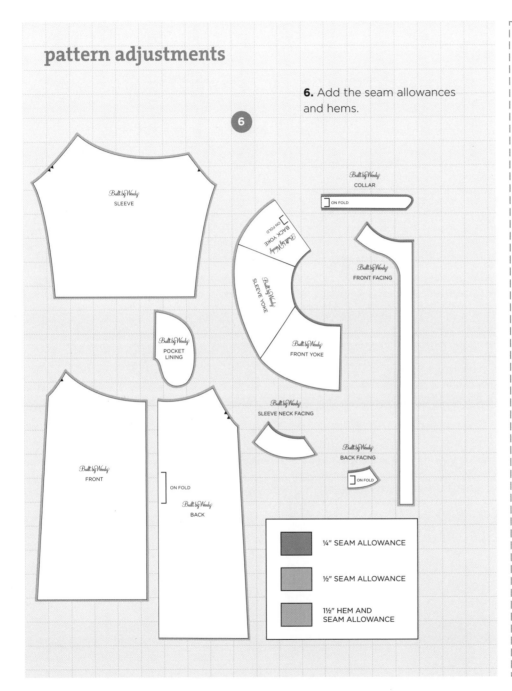

6

Built by Wendy
SLEEVE

Built by Wendy
COLLAR

ON FOLD

Built by Wendy
BACK YOKE
ON FOLD

Built by Wendy
SLEEVE YOKE

Built by Wendy
FRONT FACING

Built by Wendy
POCKET LINING

Built by Wendy
FRONT YOKE

Built by Wendy
SLEEVE NECK FACING

Built by Wendy
FRONT

ON FOLD

Built by Wendy
BACK

Built by Wendy
BACK FACING

ON FOLD

⬛	¼" SEAM ALLOWANCE
⬛	½" SEAM ALLOWANCE
⬛	1½" HEM AND SEAM ALLOWANCE

ALTERNATIVE

Frou Season

The curved yoke shape also makes an ideal place to insert a ruffle. I like this pattern in cotton chambray (just one color this time!) with ruffles inserted into the yoke, sleeve openings, and neckline; it's feminine and festive, but the straight, simple silhouette and blue-collar fabric keeps the overall vibe casual and not too froufrou. It's a fun way to spice up a pair of khakis, and a great alternative to a lightweight trench!

cutting

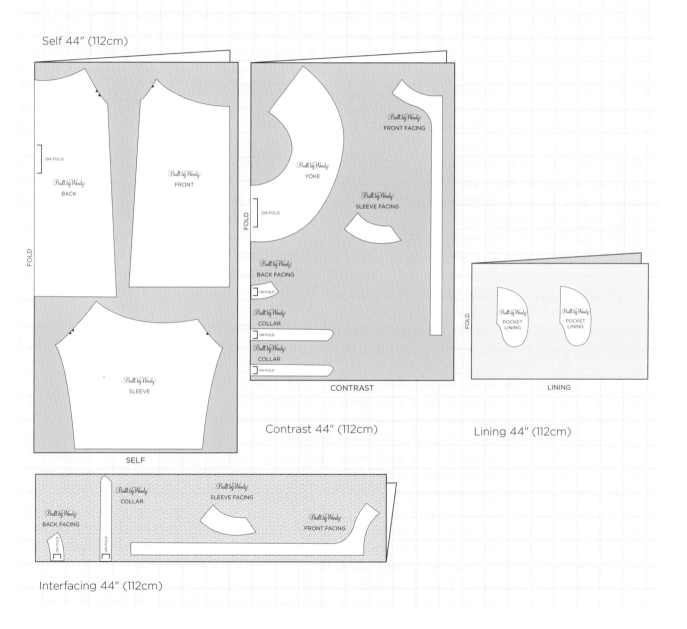

Self 44" (112cm)

ON FOLD

Built by Wendy
BACK

FOLD

Built by Wendy
FRONT

FOLD

Built by Wendy
SLEEVE

SELF

Built by Wendy
YOKE

Built by Wendy
FRONT FACING

FOLD

ON FOLD

Built by Wendy
SLEEVE FACING

Built by Wendy
BACK FACING

ON FOLD

Built by Wendy
COLLAR

ON FOLD

Built by Wendy
COLLAR

ON FOLD

CONTRAST

Contrast 44" (112cm)

FOLD

Built by Wendy
POCKET LINING

Built by Wendy
POCKET LINING

LINING

Lining 44" (112cm)

Built by Wendy
COLLAR

Built by Wendy
SLEEVE FACING

Built by Wendy
BACK FACING

ON FOLD

ON FOLD

Built by Wendy
FRONT FACING

Interfacing 44" (112cm)

sewing

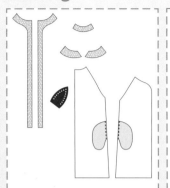

1. Attach the interfacing to the collar and facings.

2. With right sides together, sew the pocket lining pieces to the front and back pieces along the side seams.

3. With right sides together, sew the front body to the front sleeve edges and the back body to the back sleeve edges.

4. With right sides together, sew thè yoke to the body.

5. With right sides together, sew the front to the back along the side seams from the bottom opening up to the sleeve opening, sewing around the pocket linings.

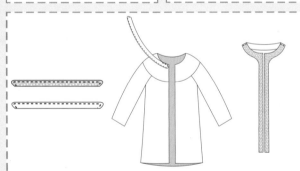

6. With right sides together, sew the collar pieces together around the sides and outer edge. Turn it right side out and topstitch.

7. With right sides together, sew the collar to the neckline, beginning at the center back.

8. With right sides together, sew the front, sleeve, neck, and back facings together.

9. With right sides together, sew the facing to the body, sandwiching the collar. Turn the facing right side out and understitch.

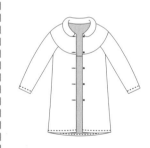

10. Hem the sleeve and bottom openings.

11. Attach the buttons and make buttonholes, spacing them equally from 1″ (2.5cm) below the neck to 4″ (10cm) above the bottom opening.

A FRESH COAT: *IDEAS FOR REMAKING OUTERWEAR*

Sure, you're probably bursting with ideas for how to make a whole wardrobe of new coats and jackets. But what about the dreary old barn jacket or vintage cashmere coat in your hall closet? As it turns out, existing coats and jackets are fun—and surprisingly easy—to work with too, and they can be modified to create exciting new styles. Since many existing coats and jackets have linings, remember to consider that layer when making sewing adjustments.

ADJUSTING SIZE

It's easy to make a big coat smaller. It's not really possible to make a small coat bigger. Luckily, there are a lot of ways to shrink a big coat. The main approaches are to simply hem it, or to create new seams to shrink the body.

Good makeover candidates: Anything that has basic style elements (collar, fabric, hardware) you love but just doesn't fit; anything with an exaggerated-shoulder raglan sleeve (easy to skim down)

Risky business: Trying to rework eighties-style pleated shoulders and set-in armholes (reconstructing a shoulder and armhole area is for experts only); messing with existing darts and curved shaping seams

Overall Shortening

Boxy jackets can look really cool when they're cropped, so why not take Dad's Burberry trench and hem it at waist height? A dowdy long overcoat with giant shoulder pads, à la Diane Keaton in *Baby Boom*, could be really modern if it hit at the hip.

Sleeve Shortening

You can also adjust sleeve length. An A-line coat can look really fresh with short sleeves; you can remove the sleeves of a leather bomber to create a cool, slouchy vest. To make these changes, simply hem the area as you normally would.

Downsize!

How best to shrink a coat's overall shape depends on the jacket's construction, but you can make a coat smaller by following existing seams. This is a good idea if you simply want to skim something down; either try it on and pin the sides, or trace the outline of a favorite jacket on top).

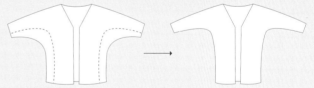

Details

It's not just the fit of an old coat that needs help sometimes. The details can be cut down too. For instance, if you hate the pockets on a peacoat, you can always remove them, cut a new shape, and reattach them—or just leave them off!

resources

moodfabrics.com
As seen on *Project Runway*—need I say more? One of the best sources for designer-caliber specialty fabrics.

voguefabricsstore.com
I grew up going to the Evanston, Illinois branch of this Chicago-area mini-chain with my mom, and all of my first projects were made from fabrics found here. It's still a great resource for all sorts of fabrics, many offered wholesale.

bandjfabrics.com
A popular store in NYC for higher-end European fabrics as well as the basics.

peakfabrics.com
A Seattle-based site specializing in technical outerwear fabrics, like ripstop nylon, neoprene, and suede sherpa fleece.

seattlefabrics.com
They know their outerwear in the Pacific Northwest! Another great stop for hi-tech specialty textiles, like Gore-Tex shell fabric and camo-print faux suede.

mjtrim.com
Whether it's piping, ribbon, buttons, or appliqués, you'll find plenty of bells and whistles here to make your design unique.

clotilde.com
A staple site of mine for sewing supplies—presser feet, needles, you name it.

ebay.com
A gold mine for one-of-a-kind vintage fabric, as well as cut-price supplies and machinery. If you want it, it's probably on here somewhere!

denverfabrics.com
This discount site has a particularly wide array of wools, and the price is right.

hancockfabrics.com
This national chain, found in most cities, sells a wide array of fabrics as well as essential extras like interfacing.

steinlaufandstoller.com
NYC-based store for professional-caliber trims and supplies, including specialty doodads like webbing, belt backing, and lingerie sliders.

joann.com
An old standby, this chain found throughout the U.S. stocks a variety of fabrics and trims.

gorgeousfabrics.com
A site beloved by sewing bloggers for its fun, colorful prints and plaids aplenty.

tessuti-shop.com
Based in Australia, this store sells fabrics bought from the world's top designers.

lanetzliving.com
This site sells loads of amazing vintage patterns—use them to add elements to the patterns in this book, or simply browse for inspiration!

antiquefabric.com
The beautiful fabrics on this site date back to the 19th century and are mostly lighter in weight, but many could make for a one-of-a-kind lining.

fabrictales.com
This site specializes in Japanese fabrics and trims with vibrant color and detail. The patterned cords, ribbons, and beads are also super-inspiring.

nearseanaturals.com
Geared to home sewers who want to go green, this site has fabrics and notions made with organic cotton, and even some hard-to-find organic wools for coats.

glossary

backstitch A few stitches in reverse, sewn at the beginning and end of a seam, to secure the threads. Most machines have a button to activate this automatically, or you can do it by hand by turning your hand wheel away from you.

bartack A back-and-forth stitch used to attach a belt loop or secure a perpendicular line of stitching.

basting stitch A stitch of long stitch length used not to join seams permanently, but to secure fabric in preparation for joining. This stitching is often removed after sewing, but not always. Ruffles and zippers will use this method.

bias The imaginary line formed at a 45-degree angle from the lengthwise and crosswise grains of woven fabric. This is where fabric stretches the most.

bias binding Also known as bias tape. A thin strip of fabric cut on the bias, used to envelop the raw edge of a hem or seam. It can be bought prepackaged or homemade from your own fabric and scraps. A bias tape maker helps speed that process.

blind hem A hem that is virtually invisible from the outside of a garment because the thread only pricks the surface occasionally. A special foot is required to accomplish this. Not recommended for beginners.

blocking The process of straightening fabric by pulling it so that lengthwise and crosswise grains meet at a 90-degree angle before sewing.

bobbin A tiny spool inserted inside the machine, usually underneath the needle hole, that holds thread. The bobbin thread links with the needle thread to form each stitch.

crosswise grain The direction of fabric weave that runs from selvage to selvage, or "horizontally." Also known as the weft.

dart A small pie-shaped marking on a pattern that is sewed into a tuck to give shape to a pattern to better fit the contours of the body.

edgestitch A line of stitching run extremely close to a folded edge or a seam line. Produces a neater, dressier look and is usually sewn with a shorter stitch length.

extension A functional extra piece on a coat or jacket closure. Extensions may be used to cover zipper openings, or may themselves hold the closure hardware (such as buttons or snaps).

facing Pieces that are mirror images of pattern pieces. Commonly used to finish openings such as necklines, front shirt openings, and armholes. Linings are also facings.

grainline Generally speaking, this refers to the lengthwise grain—the direction of the weave that runs parallel to the selvage and the most important and strongest direction of the weave.

grainline arrows These mark the direction of the grainline on patterns to indicate where on the fabric in relation to the grainline the pattern pieces should be placed.

hem A common method of finishing a raw edge by turning it under twice and stitching.

interfacing A special layer of fabric, not visible from the outside, joined to the back of fabric to support delicate and detailed areas such as collars, cuffs, and pockets. Comes in sew-on and fusible varieties; fusible interfacing is simply ironed to the back of the fabric.

glossary

lengthwise grain The direction of fabric weave that runs parallel to the selvage, or "vertically," and is the strongest direction of the fabric. Also known as the warp.

muslin Usually made of cotton, this is an inexpensive fabric used to make test garments before sewing with more precious material.

nap The raised surface of a fabric that changes appearance when brushed or viewed from different angles. Napped fabrics, unlike regular fabrics, must always be cut in the same direction.

notions Everything you use to sew that isn't fabric or trim—needles, thread, interfacing, buttons, zippers, and the like. It's best to stock up on notions so you won't need to run out and buy something specific at the sewing store every time you start a new project.

one-way fabrics Fabrics that have a nap or a special print, and thus must be cut in one direction only.

pinking Finishing an edge with pinking shears, which produces a zigzag cut and prevents many fabrics from fraying. This is the easiest way to finish a seam.

placket An opening or slit. In this book, it refers to the opening above a sleeve's cuff.

presser foot The changeable device on a sewing machine that holds the fabric in place during sewing. Special presser feet are required for specific tasks such as sewing a zipper.

princess seams Curved seams on the front of a coat or jacket that provide shaping to accommodate the bust.

right side/wrong side The right side of fabric is the side designed to be seen. The wrong side is the "back." However, you may choose to use the wrong side as a design accent, or even make a garment with the wrong side out. If so, designate it the "right" side for the purposes of the instructions in this book. Pieces are often sewn "face to face," which means right side to right side.

rotary cutter and mat A wheel-shaped blade used to cut pattern pieces quickly and efficiently with less strain on the wrist. Must be used with a self-healing mat to prevent damage to the surface beneath.

seam A line of stitching that joins two pieces of fabric.

seam allowance The area in between the edge of the cut piece and the line where the seam goes. In this book, it is ½" (13mm) for most areas and ¼" (6mm) for small areas such as necklines. Seam allowances are built into the patterns in this book, but if you alter the shape of the pattern, you must take a seam allowance into account.

seam ripper A small tool used to tear open seams without cutting into fabric.

selvage The finished side edges of a bolt of fabric.

serger A type of sewing machine that uses multiple spools of thread to sew, trim, and finish seams simultaneously. Used to make professional-quality knits. Not for beginners.

shank The stem of a button.

staystitch A basting stitch applied along the seam allowance. Sewn to a piece before joining it to another piece to stabilize delicate areas and prevent stretching.

thread tension The balance between the needle and bobbin threads in a stitch. If one of the threads pulls with more tension than the other,

biographies

the stitch will not meet in the center of the fabric. Must be calibrated before sewing a garment.

topstitch A stitch sewn about ¼" (6mm) from seam allowance edge, with the right side of fabric facing up during sewing. Can be functional or decorative.

understitch When a seam allowance is folded over and hidden inside facing, this stitch joins the seam allowance to the facing. The wrong side of fabric faces up during sewing.

warp Also known as the lengthwise grain or grainline. Runs parallel to selvage and is the strongest direction of the fabric.

weft Also known as the crosswise grain. Runs from selvage to selvage.

yoke A shaped panel of fabric that is topstitched onto or inserted into a garment for decorative or shaping purposes.

zigzag stitch A Z-shaped stitch that allows for more stretch and is thus used for knits. Tight zigzag stitches form buttonholes and appliqué borders.

WENDY MULLIN

Wendy Mullin is the designer behind the label Built by Wendy, established in 1991. She is a self-taught sewer and patternmaker with over 25 years of experience. She lives and works in New York City. For more information about Wendy, visit her website, www.builtbywendy.com

EVIANA HARTMAN

Collaborating with Wendy on the writing of the *Sew U* books made Eviana Hartman so excited about sewing that she started her own clothing line, Bodkin, in 2008. Eviana was previously an eco-columnist for *The Washington Post*, the fashion features editor at *NYLON*, and a fashion writer at *Vogue* and *Teen Vogue*, and has also written for *Dwell, I.D., Purple Fashion*, and *Wired.* She lives and works in Brooklyn, New York, and also plays drums in her free time.

BECI ORPIN

Beci Orpin is a designer-illustrator based in Melbourne, Australia. She has been working freelance for over 10 years and her clients include Universal Music, Visa, Foster's, and Mercedes-Benz. In addition to freelance work, Beci also exhibits her work frequently and runs the children's clothing label Tiny Mammoth. When she is not working, Beci likes riding her bike, gardening, and hanging out with her two sons, Tyke and Ari, and partner, Raph. For more information about Beci, visit her website at www.beciorpin.com

DANA VACCARELLI

Dana Vaccarelli graduated from the School of Visual Arts in 2007, and works as a graphic designer at Built by Wendy in New York City. She loves her job, but admits that she's mainly in it for the clothes. For more about Dana, visit her website at www.danavaccarelli.com.

index